"Platform" is the word tha writer's heart quake. (And lo shaken!) Tackling everything from social media to pre-sales, Kate and Shannon look at platform-building practices with a biblical lens that will calm our trembling heart. This book helps to transfer our confidence in our messages to Christ once and for all. *Influence* has given us a Scriptural foundation on which our platform can be safely built.

Amy Carroll
Proverbs 31 Ministries speaker and writer, author, and Next Step Coaching Services speaking coach

Cheri Gregory
Author, speaker, and Write Beside You writing coach

Today's author faces pressure like never before to plug, push, and promote her own work. This is difficult for most writers, who'd rather craft books than sell them, and even more so for the Christian called to self-forgetfulness over self-promotion. How can we play our part in the contemporary publishing world without losing our soul?

In *Influence*, Kate Motaung and Shannon Popkin place platform building where it belongs—in the context of character and calling. Recounting their own failures, successes, and lessons alongside biblical insights, they help us navigate fear, comparison, and other perils while encouraging us to humbly share our gifts. This is a timely, helpful book reminding us that platforms are best built for the service of God and others.

Sheridan Voysey
Writer, broadcaster, and author of *The Making of Us: Who We Can Become When Life Doesn't Go as Planned* and *Resurrection Year: Turning Broken Dreams into New Beginnings*

With wisdom and grace, Kate and Shannon serve as our wilderness guides, leading us through the deep valleys, treacherous terrain, and hopeful hollows we all face on the journey from fearful wanderer to front-line warrior. Real-life stories, powerful analogies, and penetrating questions energize and equip us for each new adventure while keeping our focus and priorities firmly fixed on Christ and eternal results. Read it. Share it. Live it!

Marnie Swedberg
International Leadership Mentor, www.Marnie.com

Influence is a book I didn't know I needed until I read it. Kate and Shannon give permission to use our gifts for God's glory and then show us how to focus on making a name for Jesus instead of making a name for ourselves. The authors exposed my pride, fear, and selfish motives, but through their wise mentoring and refreshing honesty, I'm emboldened to step into my calling as a woman of influence.

Leslie Bennett
Revive Our Hearts, Women's Ministry Initiatives

Influence is a much-needed resource for authors who want to steward their God-given message with prayer, impact, and purpose.

In my work with hundreds of Christian authors and publishers, their main focus remains constant: They each desire to share the Gospel in a way that honors God first and foremost over themselves.

Often the business side of marketing and selling books can create a real tension in this space between stewarding a message well and self-promotion. What I love most about *Influence* is that it offers a sigh of relief along with a balanced approach on how to address this tension with grace and confidence.

Lindsey Hartz
Marketing and Launch Consultant for Christian Authors and Publishers at Lindsey Hartz Creative

Influence is the book every Christian needs who influences or communicates through writing, speaking, or a social media platform. Shannon and Kate's honest, biblical, and refreshing perspective on the industry provides a professional compass for both new and seasoned writers and speakers. Their message reflects my own passion and struggle with ministry and marketing. Their book lets you know you're not alone in those feelings and provides a practical, biblical roadmap to share your message in today's generation. *Influence* is something I will read again and will share with those I coach and teach!

Brenda L. Yoder, LMHC
Influencer and author of
Fledge: Launching Your Kids Without Losing Your Mind

Influence

BUILDING A PLATFORM
THAT ELEVATES
JESUS
(NOT ME)

KATE MOTAUNG AND
SHANNON POPKIN

Kate
& Shannon
Col. 3:17

DEDICATION

From Kate:

To the Five Minute Friday writing community

From Shannon:

To Chris and Jamie Brauns, whose influence on my life,
for the sake of the Kingdom, has spanned decades.

CONTENTS

Dedication vii

Chapter One: **Tension** 1

Chapter Two: **Fear** 15

Chapter Three: **Calling** 23

Chapter Four: **Foreword** 31

Chapter Five: **Strategy** 43

Chapter Six: **Pride** 55

Chapter Seven: **Compare** 69

Chapter Eight: **Sift** 79

Chapter Nine: **Serve** 93

Chapter Ten: **Network** 103

Chapter Eleven: **Focus** 115

Chapter Twelve: **Trust** 125

Discussion Group Guide 139

Acknowledgments 149

About the Authors 152

Other Books by the Authors 153

{CHAPTER ONE}

TENSION

"For every look at yourself, take ten looks at Christ."
— *Robert Murray M'Cheyne*

Having grown up on the shores of Lake Michigan, I (Kate) have countless memories as a little girl on sunny summer afternoons, beach towel draped around my neck, gazing at the sparkling water that called my name. I would kick off my flip flops as soon as my feet hit the sand, often only to squeal at the burning sensation underfoot as I hightailed it down to the relief of cool water.

Most days a lighter band of water revealed a sand bar—my primary destination. I would make it there eventually, but getting from shore to sand bar meant I would have to get cold first...*really* cold. No matter how many times I went to the beach, there was still that moment of hesitation. I knew I would enjoy it as soon as my body adjusted; I just had to get over that initial shock to my system.

Sometimes becoming an influencer for the sake of the

gospel begins the same way.

Perhaps your toes are burning with the desire to get published. Or maybe you're gazing out at the goal of becoming a speaker who proclaims truth that sets people free. You've taken step after step of faith—going to conferences, offering to speak, or starting a blog. You've plodded along through the challenging journey in the sand, and you've finally arrived at the edge of your dream. You can see that shimmering sandbar not too far in the distance, beckoning you.

You bravely dip your toes into the world of being a writer or speaker, and—*splash!* You're instantly hit by the cold, crashing wave of reality: "Your platform isn't big enough." The phrase shocks your system.

You learn that even authors with high caliber book proposals and manuscripts are being turned down because they don't have enough email subscribers. You discover that even a dozen speaking engagements per year won't necessarily warrant a publisher's investment. The discouragement can be enough to make you want to throw in the beach towel, pack up your umbrella, and go back to whatever you were doing before you set foot on the sand.

But you can't. The burning sensation was not just from the hot grains under your feet—you have a burning within, a fire in your soul that refuses to be extinguished. You have a calling from God to fulfill the vision and mission He has given. You can't settle for dipping your toe and turning around. You want to be fully immersed—yet the unpleasant steps required to get there leave you doubting and deflated.

Both Shannon and I have felt it, too—that burdening need to write, speak, and lead—but also the shocking cold reality of what it will take to get there. Besides the hard work and discomfort involved with putting ourselves out there, as Christians we also face the moral dilemma that accompanies platform building. After all, doesn't the very idea of building a platform for ourselves go against what Jesus taught?

BARRIER TO ENTRY

When I first approached the shore of a writing ministry, my conscience presented a barrier that kept me from diving into the water. I wrestled with the question, *How can I exalt myself when the Bible tells me to humble myself and exalt God?* I wondered how I could reconcile the need to "build a platform" in light of passages like Philippians 2:

> "Do nothing out of selfish ambition or vain conceit. Rather, in humility value others above yourselves, not looking to your own interests but each of you to the interests of the others." (Philippians 2:3-4)

Nothing out of selfish ambition. Not looking to your own interests. Don't both of those phrases automatically disqualify personal platform building as a biblical pursuit? But that's not all; Paul, the writer of Philippians, goes on:

> "In your relationships with one another, have the same mindset as Christ Jesus: Who, being in very nature God, did not consider equality with God something to be used to his own advantage; rather, he made himself nothing by taking the very nature of a servant, being made in human likeness. And being found in appearance as a man, he humbled himself by becoming obedient to death—even death on a cross!" (Philippians 2:5-8)

As a Christian writer, how can I promote myself in good conscience when the One who "made himself nothing" calls me to imitate Him? Writer Jenn Hesse says, "Platform building seems antithetical to the gospel. I don't want to elevate myself; I want to elevate Christ." But then there's the flip side. What about passages like the following portion from Jesus' famous Sermon on the Mount?

> "You are the light of the world. A town built on a hill cannot be hidden. Neither do people light a lamp and put it under a bowl. Instead they put it on its stand, and it gives light to everyone in the house. In the same way, let your light shine before others, that they may see your good deeds and glorify your Father in heaven." (Matthew 5:14-16)

Was Jesus saying it's okay to build a platform if I'm doing it for the right reasons? If so, how can I know what those "right reasons" are? The deeper I wade into the waters of platform building, the more exhausted I feel. Is the effort worth it?

As people desiring to influence the world with the hope of the gospel, should we immerse ourselves in the work of building a platform? Should we dive wholeheartedly into the unpleasant waters of expanding our reach? Is that what *Jesus* would have us do?

FACING THE TENSION

Shannon and I are relatively new authors, with our first traditionally published books released in 2017 and 2018, respectively. We've both had to face the task of creating a "brand" and carving passageways through the digital landscape to get our messages out to the world.

We know what it's like to be relatively "unknown" influencers and to step onto a tiny platform with a big desire to please Jesus. We also know what it's like to be overwhelmed by this noisy world, where everyone is fighting to be heard. We've had the advice of countless mentors ringing in our ears: "If you want to get your message out, you're going to have to build a platform. You have to market yourself."

Both of us have particularly struggled with building platforms as Christians influencers. Is there a way to gather followers and still follow Jesus? Is there a way to both take up our cross and build up our stats? Is it possible to raise our Google rank and still elevate Christ?

We're excited to tell you that we've come to the strong and happy conclusion that there is a way. We've written this book to help you sort out some of the same questions we've wrestled with. Questions like:

- Should I seek to build a platform or just trust God?

- Is it possible to elevate my message and still be humble?

- How can I overcome the swell of fears I face every time I think about "putting myself out there"?

- Does Jesus want me to be strategic in my writing and speaking ministry?

- How can I weigh my own motives?

- Am I self-serving when I try to network?

We invite you to join us as we consider these issues from a biblical perspective. Yes, at times the journey might feel as if you're trying to run underwater—but we trust that if you stick with it to the end, you'll emerge with new confidence and decision-making clarity as you let your light shine before others to glorify your Father in heaven.

PLATFORM WITH A PURPOSE

When my (Shannon) daughter was two, my husband and I took her to a pool where a lifeguard was seated on a tall, tall chair. My daughter tipped up her little chin, gazed at the lifeguard, then said, "That's the king, isn't it Daddy?" She had mistakenly assumed that—like in her picture books—anyone positioned on an elevated chair or platform was a king.

Sometimes as adults, we make the same mistake. We assign more status and importance to well-known Christians standing on their public "platforms." For what is the purpose of a platform, if not to elevate the person standing on it? Yet for the follower of Christ, a platform should be the structure from which we serve others, not ourselves. When you and I step onto our God-given platforms, our goal should be to elevate Jesus, not ourselves. Our message should lead others to His story and glory, not our own.

Like a lifeguard ready and able to toss a buoy to someone struggling, or to call out caution to one who needs warning, we position ourselves to serve. We plant our feet in a place where we can most effectively toss out what other people need: the truth about Jesus.

DISTRIBUTING LIFE JACKETS

Jesus' self-stated mission was to seek and save the lost (Luke 19:10). He came to a world full of people drowning in their sin, and offered Himself as the only way to be saved. And now, as His ambassadors, we get to continue Jesus' work. We get to pass out life jackets to people who are lost, hurting, weary, and overwhelmed.

With such an important mission, why would we not throw out as many life jackets as possible?

Actually, what often stops us from effectively tossing life jackets is *us*. We stand in our own way. Sometimes we stop because we think we're not good enough or equipped for the task. Or maybe we feel paralyzed by fear of rejection. We think, *Nobody wants a life jacket from me. I'm sure they can get one from somebody else. Other people probably have better life jackets to offer. What if I offer a life jacket and it gets rejected?*

We not only doubt ourselves; we doubt our platforms,

too. We think, *What do I have to add? My platform is so small, my toes hang off the edge! Even if I tried, I couldn't make a difference in this ocean of need....* Out of fear, self-consciousness, and a lack of confidence we back away, hoping God will send someone else.

Other times, we can become a bit overconfident in our life jacket tossing. We get so caught up in the excitement and hype of passing out life jackets that we forget the whole point of our mission. Instead of focusing on the vast need or the purpose of the offering, we subconsciously start acting like life jacket models.

We think or even say, *Look at me! Look how great I look in my life jacket. Look how good I am at distributing these life-saving devices!* Our platforms can make us feel elevated and important. Soon we may find ourselves thinking, *I like standing up here where everyone can see me. I hope they all notice what a great life jacket model I am!*

Do you see yourself falling into either of these categories? Are you underconfident or overconfident about your role as an influencer?

THE UNDERCONFIDENT INFLUENCER

After speaking at a women's event, I (Shannon) stood near the book table—signing books, answering questions, and praying with women who needed encouragement. Eventually the line dwindled and the leaders began clearing tables and loading up centerpieces. As I wrapped up my last conversation I noticed a woman lingering nearby. We made eye contact and I could tell she wanted to talk to me, but was waiting to be last. Before she even uttered a word, I guessed her secret. She wants to be a speaker and writer.

Whenever I see that glimmer of excitement mixed with sheer terror in the eye of someone waiting to talk with me, I just *know*. Partly because I remember. I used to be the one lingering, waiting to reveal my secret to a woman up ahead on the path I longed to travel.

The words of hope and encouragement I offered this young woman were the same words others first offered to me. If you're an underconfident influencer, they're the words I'd like to offer to you:

Are you longing for permission? Do you feel that you need someone's blessing before you pursue this dream of influencing others for Jesus? If so, it's freely yours! My great delight—and Kate's, too—would be to stand with you as you bravely turn your toes toward the sea of need, position yourself with confidence on the platform of influence God has given you, and start passing out life jackets to those who will benefit.

THE OVERCONFIDENT INFLUENCER

If you're an overconfident influencer, we'd like to encourage you, too—but first, may I raise a question? I'm concerned that you might not *know* you're an overconfident influencer. That's how it works with confidence. When you have too much of it, you're often the last to know.

My friend, Carole, spent many years serving as the speaker coordinator for her large, multi-site church. She fielded countless phone calls from eager speakers hoping to be considered for an upcoming event. One such inquiry stood out from a woman named "Sheri."

Carole cut the conversation short by saying, "Thanks so much for calling, Sheri, but I don't think we have a place for you on our schedule at this time." Sheri politely expressed her gratitude, then hung up. But a few minutes later, she called Carole back.

"Can I ask you something?" asked Sheri. "I think perhaps I said something wrong. Could you help me so I don't repeat my mistake?" Notice the woman's humility? Carole noticed and was happy to help. She explained that Sheri had given the impression that she *knew* she would be a good fit. She *knew* that her message would resonate with this group. She *knew* that God would use her to produce great fruit.

But Carole explained that she (not Sheri) was the one tasked with serving this particular group of women. Carole knew the history of her church and her group's particular needs at that time. She was looking for a speaker who would listen, adapt, and be willing to serve—not someone who would rush ahead, overconfident in her own skills.

I remember when Carole first told me this story years ago. I was even more green in my writing and speaking ministry, and with raised eyebrows, I thought, *Note to self. Make sure to affirm that the coordinator is the expert regarding her own women!*

Over the years, I've learned that this involves more than just verbiage to insert into a phone call or email. It's a heart attitude. When I'm overconfident, I make the mistake of not listening or adapting to the needs around me. I get too comfortable in my role and assume my message is "ready-made" for any group.

I've also learned to adopt a certain degree of skepticism toward my own heart, for my heart is quick to deceive me (Jeremiah 17:9). It's quite easy to convince myself that I am humble and ready to serve, when really I'm too proud and relying on my own strength, not God's.

If you're pretty convinced that you have the perfect blend of confidence and humility, can I urge you to pause and contemplate? You wouldn't be the first person to be deceived by your own heart. Our hope is that you might work through this book with a healthy dose of introspection, and grow in the beauty of humility.

Friends, whether we tend toward underconfidence or overconfidence, what we've lost is perspective. As underconfident influencers, we forget that God's strength is made perfect in our weakness (2 Corinthians 12:9). As overconfident influencers, we forget that apart from Christ, we can do nothing (John 15:5). Either way, we must gain clarity on our role and God's role.

It isn't our job to build our own platforms from scratch. God asks us to build *onto* what Jesus has already accomplished. We are simply extending the reach of Christ into a dark and hurting world that desperately needs Him.

But how do we do that, exactly? Should we start with a blog? Or an Instagram account? Should we put money into a new website logo or advertising on Facebook?

YOUR DIGITAL BUY-IN

The digital age in which we live creates unique challenges. In eras gone by, writers could live anonymously. Speakers only addressed the audience in front of them. Influencers didn't leave digital footprints because the digital universe had not been discovered. But today, it's nearly impossible to influence anyone without operating online, because that's where most people have chosen to live.

If you're more of a digital introvert, the process of entering the digital world might have gone something like this: You looked up one day and realized that things had changed. (They continue to change every day, it seems.) A parallel universe had sprung up around you. Wherever you looked—in restaurants, grocery store lines, and bus stops—every person had a phone in hand. Young or old, they had earbuds and video playing.

Suddenly it dawned on you with crystal clarity (perhaps just after a rejection letter because of your small platform): In order to reach people with your message, you would *have* to step into the world they all live in: the digital realm.

But this thought made your stomach churn. You love the world where there's green grass beneath your feet as you reach into your mailbox. You loathe entering the one where you have to use a plug-in on your website to create a contact form that forwards to your email. It's overwhelming and frustrating. Couldn't you just get back to writing? Or speaking? Or influencing people in non-virtual reality?

On the other hand, if you're more of a digital extrovert, the thought of presenting yourself as an influencer online might have the opposite, thrilling effect. Perhaps you've had your blog header and personal bitmoji designed for months, just *waiting* for the chance to introduce your virtual self around digi-town.

Regardless of your online personality type, one thing is sure. Whether you drag yourself in or enter with virtual confetti, digital buy-in is necessary for those who want to influence multitudes in today's world. So you launch a blog. You begin collecting email subscribers. You set up shop on various social media platforms. You obediently step inside the online marketplace of ideas.

Then suddenly—often without you realizing—something new begins to happen. The waters of your heart's motivation begin to cloud.

MURKY WATERS

Sharing Jesus and spreading truth has never been more possible. Also, branding yourself and selling your ideas has never been more possible. And those two have become mingled more than ever before.

The digital world is one filled with links. Your audience is no longer comprised of the people who walk into a building where you'll be speaking, or who walk into a bookstore and purchase your book. Today, a person only has to click a link, and instantly they're part of your audience. That's the wonder of it all.

But here's the problem. With every bit of truth you toss out, there's a link back to *you*. Your bio. Your social profile. Your website. And every time someone clicks on those links, you know about it. The clicks become tally marks.

Counting clicks becomes a way of keeping score; a tangible way of measuring your influence.

Suddenly, with no warning, your untainted passion to serve and share and give is contaminated with self-serving desires. It's hard to separate the selfish motives from the pure. Your desire to give of yourself is permeated with a craving to receive. You long to *get* affirmation, to *gain* recognition, and to *receive* positive feedback—and you can easily become devastated, discouraged, or deflated when you *don't.*

By immersing yourself in the choppy seas of the internet, you're swimming in an environment with a forceful undertow that has pulled too many of us under—the undertow of self-interest. It runs beneath all of our efforts to serve Jesus and others. It threatens to drown out whatever influence we have. And it's far too dangerous for any of us to ignore.

So our challenge for you is: don't. Don't shrug your shoulders and sidestep the hard questions presented by the digital world. Don't allow yourself to be anchored to the fear of not measuring up. Don't let yourself be swept away by the current of affirmation. Refuse to be buried by the shifting sands of approval or the devastation of being ignored.

Instead, come join us on a stroll down the shore, led by the greatest influencer of all time. We've invited Jesus—the carpenter from Nazareth—to lead this coaching session on how to build a platform that lasts. Rather than building a platform out of sand that will be whisked away by the next wave of doubt or discouragement, let's build our efforts on the rock-solid foundation of obedience to Him. Let's be shaped by the example of Christ, the greatest servant of all.

READYING OURSELVES

Are you ready? Are you willing? We all have work to do. As

you read this book, which challenge will you be pressing yourself to overcome?

For some of us, it's the challenge of underconfidence. We need to overcome our sheepish self-consciousness and find the courage to bravely step onto our platforms. For others of us, it's the challenge of overconfidence. We need to learn to guard against showy self-focus and stop acting like life jacket models. Perhaps some of us struggle both ways. We vacillate between wanting to hide under a rock and secretly longing to be a rock star.

The key to finding balance isn't learning to keep our feet in the middle of the pier, but rather in lifting our eyes, scanning the waves, and keeping watch for victims who are drowning. As we lift our gaze—either from our toes or our stats—and refocus on a world full of people who need the hope of Christ, the cloudiness dissipates and our mission as influencers becomes clear: We are meant to serve others, not ourselves.

With every post, tweet, and microphone, we have the opportunity to stand firmly on the platform first laid by the cross of Christ. We get to toss life jackets to people who need to be saved! We get to toss out buoys of hope to those who are exhausted, fearful, and disoriented.

Kate and I are honored to have you with us on this journey. Our hope is that by the time you reach the end of this book, you'll be inspired enough, convicted enough, and emboldened enough to speak—not your message, but His.

{CHAPTER TWO}

FEAR

"When I am afraid, I put my trust in you."
— *Psalm 56:3*

Whenever I (Kate) interact with Christian writers and speakers about the notion of self-promotion and building a platform, the conversation turns to one common theme: *Fear*. It comes in countless shapes, colors, and sizes, but it's always there.

I've faced several fears while writing this very chapter. Fears like: Will people look at my online efforts more critically after reading this book? Will they think I'm a fraud or a hypocrite if I post something online that seems to contradict the message I'm trying to share here? Will I be judged for my success or lack thereof? Will readers see how small my platform is and laugh or roll their eyes?

One day I asked the following question on Twitter: "What is your biggest challenge/fear/roadblock/secret regarding platform building as a writer, speaker, or influencer?"[1] I was so surprised by the volume of responses, including:

- The fear of being misunderstood

- The fear of being rejected

- The fear of being ridiculed

- The fear of failure

- The fear of being wrongly perceived

- The fear of focusing too much on self

- The fear of getting caught up in the numbers

- The fear of not being popular enough

- The fear of not having anything new or interesting or important enough to say

- The fear of silence from the audience

- The fear of seeming self-consumed

- …and countless more iterations

Can you relate? Are you terrified to put your heart out there for all to see, to expose yourself to the possibility of criticism, harsh responses, and misunderstanding? What if something you say or do leaves people with a negative impression of you? What if you unwittingly develop a reputation you didn't want? What if you offend someone? What if a reader or listener unfriends you or stops following you on social media because of something you said or wrote?

What if you spend hours, days, weeks, or months of your life striving for a goal that never becomes reality? What if you spend money investing in coaching and training, and don't see the results you desire?

And one of the most sobering fears of all: What if we

do all these things in the name of serving the Lord, but end up with twisted and distorted motives that lead us down a path of spiritual destruction? After all, "the heart is deceitful above all things, and desperately sick; who can understand it?" (Jeremiah 17:9) Can we trust ourselves to know if and when we're veering off track?

What if our earthly plans to build a platform *do* succeed, and we end up puffed up, proud, and consumed with ourselves? As author Kendall Vanderslice admits, "I'm well aware of my own pride and I fear how a large following could get to my head." What if we gain the whole world and forfeit our soul? (Matthew 16:26; Mark 8:36)

These are serious, scary questions to ask—but important ones. Essential, even. We *must* ask the Lord to search our hearts every step of the way.

FIGHTING FEAR

When I pause to reflect on my own fears, I'm embarrassed to admit that I see a common theme permeating each one—the fear of people. Though I'm passionate about serving people, I'm also afraid of what they will think of me, how they will react, what they will say in response. Then I remember Jesus' words to His disciples in John 16:33: "In this world you will face trouble." As a follower of Christ, I should expect to face resistance and criticism in this life. In fact, if I'm not facing some kind of backlash for proclaiming truth, I should probably wonder whether I'm doing it right.

It's an ongoing battle, and most likely will be until the day I die—which is why it's so important for me to continually arm myself with the truths of Scripture.

When my fear of people rises or I receive a negative comment or review, I cling to Psalm 118:6-7: "The Lord is on my side; I will not fear. What can man do to me? The Lord is on my side as my helper; I shall look in triumph on those who hate me."

Paul's words in Galatians 1:10 are often convicting to me, and a good measuring stick for me to use whenever I post something online: "For am I now seeking the approval of man, or of God? Or am I trying to please man? If I were still trying to please man, I would not be a servant of Christ."

Instead of writing or speaking to please others, Colossians 3:23-24 reminds me, "Whatever you do, work heartily, as for the Lord and not for men, knowing that from the Lord you will receive the inheritance as your reward. You are serving the Lord Christ." It's the Lord's approval that you and I must seek. He has called us, He has equipped us, He will sustain us, and He is the One who can give us the only reward that matters.

When we take time to realign our thinking, to remember who it is we are serving, and to adopt a biblical perspective of our identity in Christ, many of our fears will fall away and it becomes much easier to combat "Imposter Syndrome" when it whispers in our ear.

IMPOSTER SYNDROME

I've experienced it often—that sinking feeling that I'm not qualified to even open my mouth. *Who am I to think I have anything worthwhile to say? Why should people listen to me? I'm certainly no expert!*

According to an October 2015 New York Times article online, the term for this phenomenon was assigned quite a while ago. "Two American psychologists, Pauline Clance and Suzanne Imes, gave it a name in 1978: the impostor syndrome. They described it as a feeling of 'phoniness in people who believe that they are not intelligent, capable or creative despite evidence of high achievement.' While these people 'are highly motivated to achieve,' they also 'live in fear of being 'found out' or exposed as frauds.'"[2]

The Harvard Business Review describes it this way: "Imposter syndrome can be defined as a collection of feelings of inadequacy that persist despite evident success. 'Imposters' suffer from chronic self-doubt and a sense of intellectual fraudulence that override any feelings of success or external proof of their competence. They seem unable to internalize their accomplishments, however successful they are in their field. High achieving, highly successful people often suffer, so imposter syndrome doesn't equate with low self-esteem or a lack of self-confidence."[3]

Imposter syndrome shows no discrimination between unbelievers and believers in Christ. All are susceptible to its nagging voice. But Christians have an advantage—we can combat the persistent whispers of imposter syndrome with the truth of who we are in Christ. If you belong to Him, you are in Him and He is in you. This is a profound reality that can and should shift our entire outlook on life, including our response to fear and doubt.

The right perspective is to realize and admit that we *can't* do it on our own. That we *are* nothing without Him. That we *don't* have anything to say without His enabling. Humility is essential for the people of God. It's a good thing to think less of ourselves. But it's not biblical or honoring to the Lord if we doubt His ability to use us for His purposes and His glory.

Whenever we say or think we're not equipped for the task at hand, we're not just doubting our own ability— we're doubting God's provision. We're displaying our lack of trust in His ability to work in and through us. We've placed our trust solely on ourselves to perform, succeed, and achieve in our own strength. But if He has called us, He has also equipped us. And He not only goes before us, He goes with us, because He is in us.

The Apostle Paul understood: "For this I toil, struggling with all his energy that he powerfully works within me"

(Colossians 1:29). We don't toil with our own energy or strength. It's God's strength that enables us, and His power is made perfect in our weakness (2 Corinthians 12:9).

A NEW IDENTITY

Throughout the process of writing my memoir, imposter syndrome frequently visited my heart. It came as I hunkered down in a cubicle at my local library, just settling in for a few hours of work in front of my computer: *Why are you wasting your time on this? Do you really think anyone cares about your story? You don't have anything new or interesting to say.*

It showed up in full force as I sat alone at Starbucks, accompanied only by my laptop and chai latte: *Who says you can write? Haven't you read any actual books? Yours is garbage compared to real authors.* It almost choked me when I had to send out endorsement requests to authors and leaders I have long admired and respected. Acidic bile churned in my stomach and rose in my throat as I clicked "send" on the initial ask: *Why in the world would anyone want to read this so-called book? I can't believe you just asked someone with that much influence to spend their time reviewing your work. They're going to scoff at your lack of skill! Besides, don't you know they have much better, more important things to do?*

In a talk she delivered at the Refine Retreat for Writers in 2018, author Kris Camealy admitted her own frequent struggle with imposter syndrome. Kris shared Ephesians 2:10, which says, "For we are his workmanship, created in Christ Jesus for good works, which God prepared beforehand…." She went on to give this charge to the Christian writers, speakers, and influencers present at the retreat:

> "We can best show up for the work God has prepared for us, for the art He has seeded in us, by claiming who we are in Christ. We are His, a royal

priesthood. We are prophets and teachers. The very Spirit of God Himself lives IN us. We are not imposters. You are not an imposter. You are qualified to do the work because of the shed blood of Jesus, who when He stretched His arms wide open on the cross exchanged our old identity for a new one.

You are not who you once were. You are a new creation, created in Christ Jesus for good works. *For good words.* Which, by the way, God already has prepared for you. Beforehand. Ask Him for those words and write them in the confidence that you are yourself, a masterpiece, with the blood of the Lion coursing in your veins."[4]

If I had remembered this truth that Kris presented about who I am in Christ, and if I had placed my confidence in His ability to work in and through me despite my many weaknesses, that nagging voice of imposter syndrome would have been silenced. After all, if God has given me an assignment—a work that He prepared in advance for me to do—then surely He will also equip me for the task and bring it to completion as He sees fit. The same goes for you. If you have placed your faith and trust in the Lord Jesus Christ, you have no need to fear what other people will think of you. You don't need to stand at the edge of the water, agonizing over whether you should take the next step or what will happen if you do. You are an ambassador of the Most High, and you are on His mission. Your job is to be faithful to the tasks God has prepared in advance for you to do, to be obedient to His Word and calling on your life, and to release your "good words," and trust the Lord to do His work.

"He who calls you is faithful; he will surely do it" (1 Thessalonians 5:24).

{CHAPTER THREE}

CALLING

"He who calls you is faithful; he will surely do it."
— 1 Thessalonians 5:24

About twenty years ago, when I (Shannon) was expecting my first baby, I traveled from Wisconsin to visit my parents in Michigan. After a lovely visit, I got on the road for the four-hour trek back home.

About ninety minutes into my trip, I was suddenly startled by another driver on the highway. He was honking his horn and waving wildly from the center lane. From my spot in the right lane, I immediately became cautious and guarded. Keeping my eyes straight ahead on the road in front of me, I thought, "I am doing nothing wrong here! I'm just driving in a straight line, minding my own business. What is this crazy person's problem? Why can't he leave me alone?"

This is often how I feel about people who make a lot of noise on social media. I roll my eyes when I see the same post for the seventh time in one day. I groan in irritation when I get added to yet another list that I have to manually unsubscribe from. With new caution and guardedness, I think, "What is this crazy person's problem? Why can't he leave me alone?"

That crazy highway driver, however, was not about to leave me alone. He persisted with his honking and wild waving motions, until I chanced it and made a glance in his direction.

"Dad?" I said in an incredulous tone.

The crazy driver was my father.

I quickly took the next exit and pulled off the highway into a parking lot. My dad drove up beside me with a big grin on his face. He had been chasing me down for the past seventy miles or so, trying to catch up.

This happened before I had a cell phone. And it happened *after* a lifetime of my parents bringing me things that I had left behind or forgotten. What had I left behind this time? My entire collection of maternity clothes—hanging neatly in the closet.

A NEW PERSPECTIVE

My dad knew that I wouldn't have anything to wear and wouldn't be able to afford a whole new wardrobe for the remaining weeks of my pregnancy. Without a moment's hesitation, he had torn off after me. After more than an hour of chasing me, remarkably, he was still grinning. What a great dad he is.

As you can imagine, I had a whole new perspective on that "crazy driver" in the next lane who was making noise and waving his arms. I now saw him as kind, compassionate, and incredibly considerate.

He had a message that he knew I needed to hear. He possessed something he knew I needed to receive. He was completely unconcerned about disturbing my peaceful drive or drawing attention to himself. He was actually being selfless as he made all of that noise on the highway.

So it is when we share good news about Jesus in a noisy world of ideas. There is traffic everywhere, and distractions abound. Click here! Swipe there! The world fills every moment with mind-numbing, addicting superficiality. If ever we are to be heard above the noise, we've got to make some noise ourselves!

Just think about what we have to offer. We have in our possession something much more important than clothes. We hold life! We know the secret! On the highways of life, we're surrounded by people who are lost, desperate, and spiritually dead. How ludicrous for us to shrink back in embarrassment and let them drive on by. How heartless and evil for us to stay quiet, not wanting to be perceived as crazy!

On the other hand, how absurd we look when suddenly we begin honking and waving—not out of selfless concern, but with life jacket-modeling pride. We really *are* crazy, if we've suddenly forgotten the true nature of our mission.

SELF-FORGETFULNESS

Our calling as Christian influencers is to risk it all. We might be perceived as noisy and offensive or backward and unclassy as we say things that no one else is saying—things like, "No, all roads *don't* lead to heaven," and, "Yes, some paths *do* lead to eternal destruction." Other drivers might refuse to give us a sideways glance. Or worse, turn to us with road rage.

But with an untiring grin and compelled by the urgent situation at hand, we must be undeterred. We must be like Paul, who labored tirelessly so that, "…by all means I might save some" (1 Corinthians 9:22).

Judy Dunagan, an acquiring editor for Moody Publishers, mentioned something in conversation that has left me pondering for months. She spoke of a staff meeting in which their Publisher said, "One day we might not enjoy the freedom of press that we have today. This makes our work in the Christian publishing industry even more urgent. For what if the books being produced today are all that is available to sustain the Church for generations to come?"

What a sobering thought. When I picture a Christian woman fifty years from now with one of my books hidden in her coat, I have new gravity about what should be included in that book—and less concern over the noise I have to make to get my message out into the world.

Take a moment and scan the world from where you sit. Glance around at the people driving past with their windows up and their air conditioning on—with no earthly idea of the peril that awaits. Look at what's down the road for those who are Christians, and for those who aren't. Forget about yourself for a moment and think of *them*.

In his book, *The Freedom of Self-Forgetfulness,* Tim Keller writes, "The essence of gospel humility is not thinking more of myself or thinking less of myself, it is thinking of myself less."

As we expand our platforms to fulfill God's calling on our lives, what would happen if we practiced self-forgetfulness? What if we thought of our public image less frequently? What if we worried less about how we're being perceived? What if we waved our arms, not in an attention-seeking way, but out of concern for others?

That day on the highway, my dad was not thinking of himself at all. He had one goal and one mission, and it had nothing to do with himself. As carriers of the gospel, this is our calling, too! Oh, that we would find the freedom of self-forgetfulness as we buckle up and head onto the noisy highways of life.

Self-forgetfulness helps us to see more clearly what God is calling us to do. Especially since our callings often involve cost.

ESTHER'S CALLING

Esther was a Jewish orphan who became a queen. Her story displayed the beauty of self-forgetfulness when she risked her life to gain an audience with her husband, the king. She set aside her own self-absorption and fears and became laser-focused on one thing: the impending destruction of her people.

The evil Haman had devised a plan to destroy the Jews right under the king's nose. Someone needed to speak up about it! But Esther? A young girl? A queen? She would have to disclose her identity as one of God's people. Her risk included not only being exposed, but also being beheaded!

Yet her cousin Mordecai persuaded her, saying, "For if you remain silent at this time, relief and deliverance for the Jews will arise from another place, but you and your father's family will perish. And who knows but that you have come to your royal position for such a time as this?" (Esther 4:14)

With all of God's people fasting and praying, Esther bravely and wisely used her influence with the king. She risked it all, made some noise, and kept destruction from falling on her people.

Like Esther, God has positioned you to speak for Him. Yes, there is cost involved. And yes, you can refuse. If you choose to remain silent at this time, relief and deliverance for God's people will arise from another place. But like Esther, who knows? Perhaps you have been strategically placed for such a time as this! Perhaps God has a role for you that is part of his overarching story.

Is God asking you to share your message with millions?

Or like Esther, is He asking you to bravely speak to one? Is He calling you to speak out against some evil? Or to disclose some hidden atrocity? One thing is sure. God has a call on your life. He has a purpose for you.

He has good works prepared in advance for you—in particular—to do (Ephesians 2:10). Will you remain silent? Or will you speak?

UNUSED GIFTS

Several years ago just before Christmas, I (Kate) was at the Dollar Store with my six-year-old son. "Don't watch me, Mom," he pleaded. He wanted to perform his secret mission all on his own.

I complied and did my best to give him the privacy he requested, making sure I could still see the top of his head over the store displays. I saw him lingering in the kitchen utensil aisle, but turned my back as he approached the checkout and proudly gave his savings to the cashier. Mission accomplished. I had no idea what he had bought.

When Christmas morning arrived, my fidgety boy watched with a gleam in his eye as I unwrapped his gift to me.

"A flour sifter!" I exclaimed. "How did you know?" I had never owned one before.

"Well, I looked in the kitchen to see what you had, then I looked at the store to see what you didn't have, and that's what I picked!" my son answered.

About six weeks later, my boy came to me in the kitchen and asked, "Mom, why haven't you been using your flour sifter?"

"Well…" I floundered. "I haven't really made many recipes that needed it." I watched as disappointment covered my son's face. "I'll try to come up with something soon that I could bake," I added hastily. He shuffled away, hunched shoulders unsatisfied.

This deflated, pint-sized image helped me realize what it looks like to God when we neglect to use the gifts we've been given.

If you are a child of God, you've been given gifts. Meaningful gifts. Significant gifts. Gifts that were hand-selected *just for you*. Gifts like teaching, evangelism, wisdom, shepherding, and serving (1 Corinthians 12, Ephesians 4:11-12) that have been given to you for the common good (1 Corinthians 12:7). That means God intends for your gifts to be used and shared! Left in the back of a kitchen drawer, our gifts are useless. They benefit no one, and the One who gave the gift is dishonored.

If your gift is sitting unopened in some dusty cupboard of your heart, that means God's people are not receiving what is intended for them. It's time to reach for your gift, open it up, and share it with those who will benefit.

CALLED TO GIVE

Have you ever wondered, *What is my calling?* Have you wished that you could take a peek at that list of good works that God has prepared in advance for His people to do, and find your name next to a task or two? (Ephesians 2:10)

Friend, you'll discover your calling as you open your gift and begin to use it; not before.

It's so easy to talk ourselves out of this, isn't it? We worry that by using our gifts, we come across as prideful—as if we're saying, "Hey, look at *my* gift. Look what *I* can do!"

We also worry about looking foolish. We talk ourselves out of gift-sharing, saying, "I'm not really that gifted. Other people can do what I do much better."

Both of these responses are void of self-forgetfulness. We've sized up our gifts from a self-serving perspective, asking, "How will this gift reflect on me?" But God wants us to take ourselves out of the equation. He wants us to view our gifts as something to *give.*

That day on the highway, my (Shannon) dad had something in his trunk that he knew I needed. As he waved his arms and honked his horn, he was completely self-forgetful—focused only on how to reach me.

You have something that other people need—and perhaps you've been given it "for such a time as this." Don't shrink back from your call. Don't refuse to use your gift. Instead, forget about yourself, focus on others, and get ready to make some noise!

{CHAPTER FOUR}

FOREWORD

"Let us run with endurance the race that is set before us,
looking unto Jesus, the author and finisher of our faith."
— Hebrews 12:1-2, NKJV

Before I (Shannon) became an author, I never knew that the little section at the beginning of a book is spelled "foreword," not "forward."

It's fine, you can laugh. In my defense, I never took Book Writing 101. I always assumed this was the section where the author looked "forward" and let you know what the book was going to be about.

Now that I'm a bona fide author, I've learned that a foreword is the section in which someone gives a **word** about what came be**fore** the book. Often the foreword provides us with a bit of backstory. How did this story or material evolve? What prompted the author to write it? Why is he or she the right person to share this with us?

In most cases, a foreword is written by someone other

than the author. Usually, it's a prominent person with expertise who sets up the book by giving it credibility.

YOUR FOREWORD

So, how does *your* foreword read? I'm not talking about the foreword for your latest book. I'm talking about the foreword for your ministry as a whole. I want to encourage you to think through what led you to the place you currently stand. What came be**fore** this chapter?

Before you decide to skip this section on "forewords," hold up. I know you picked up this book looking for guidance as you step *forward*, not for help reflecting on the past. But sometimes taking a glance backward can offer clarity like nothing else as you step out to do something new.

Take a look back over your shoulder. Whether you've only dipped a toe into a new venture, or you're completely immersed, something prompted you to move in this direction. Something stirred your heart. Something compelled you to put effort and resources into this dream. Even the desire to share this message with the world was likely prompted by some experience or person. How did it all begin for you?

Here are three questions to help you consider the "foreword" to your writing or speaking ministry:

- What stirred you to share your message?

- Who affirmed you?

- What doors did God swing open?

In a moment, I'll be asking you to grab some paper and write your own responses to those questions, but to get you thinking, let me share a bit of my "foreword" with you.

MY "FOREWORD"

If you look at my current bio, you'll read something like,

> "As a speaker and writer, Shannon blends her love
> for humor and storytelling with her passion for the
> truth of God's Word."

At age 47, I can say confidently that God has gifted me to tell stories—often funny ones, and use analogies to help people gain fresh perspective on and direction from God's Word. Listen to what one reader shared with me after finishing my Bible study:

> "Shannon, you have a gift. I read the Scripture as
> I went along, but you told it as if it were happen-
> ing right here and now. You told the background
> story that made it pop with richness and layers.
> Few books have rocked me in a way this one has."
> – Jaime VerLee, Life Coach

This note made my heart sing! Kind words like these reaffirm that even though I live a large portion of my life in my office—going days without showering, months without socializing, and years without any pay, I'm doing exactly what God wants me to do. This is my assignment from the Lord.

However, for the first few decades of my life, this assignment seemed rather hazy. As a child, I never said I wanted to be an author when I grew up. I never dreamed about seeing my name in print. I didn't even choose writing or communications as my college major. Admittedly, I chose to be a teacher partly because I loved telling stories. Teachers have captive audiences and can tell stories all day if they want to. And I wanted to. My stories were eating a hole in me, and I had to let them out—so my fourth graders came in handy. (They didn't want to turn to page 162 in their history books, anyway.)

I didn't realize that my stories were clues! God had planted a writer in me.

TWO MORE CLUES

In hindsight, my college years provided two additional clues about God's plans for me. The first one came when I served as a summer counselor at a Christian camp. One morning our director, Chris Brauns, said, "Hey, I listened in to that story you were telling the girls in your cabin last night."

"You *did?*" I asked, picturing him with an ear up to the screened window. He asked where the story had come from, and I explained that I made it up. For me, stories were the easiest way to get the girls to settle in, and also a great way to review that evening's chapel message. Often the girls asked for a "Part Two" and I was happy to keep the stories coming.

Chris said, "Shannon, you should consider writing! Not everyone can make up stories like that."

This was a novel idea. I had never thought of storytelling as a gift to be shared. I had simply used storytelling to my advantage—so that I could get to bed! Chris, by the way, went on to become a pastor and author, and a lifelong mentor to me. I'm not sure if I would have ever tried writing, had he not encouraged me to try.

My second clue surfaced during a class I took at Liberty University called "Literature of the Bible." There was no class I loved more, and there was no assignment I found more fulfilling or took more pride in than my final paper on the characterization of Naomi. Still today, I find such delight in digging up treasure from God's Word to write about and share with others.

A STIRRING TO WRITE

It wasn't until my mid-thirties that God first began stirring my heart to write. I taught our church's fourth through sixth graders, and spent hours preparing each week. Though I loved teaching the kids what I had learned, I loved what came afterward even more.

After putting my kids down for their Sunday afternoon nap, I would sit at the computer and write out my lesson from that morning. I would work for hours, editing and rearranging my thoughts.

My husband was puzzled. He'd say, "Remind me what you're doing, again?" He didn't understand, and honestly neither did I. Yet it felt so *good* to get the words and ideas threaded into one tidy package. Years later, I still have those lessons filed away today. They're the first little sprouts of my writing ministry.

A LONGING TO SPEAK

As a young mom, I remember listening to a woman at a retreat share a funny story about her bathrobe. I have no idea what spiritual application she was trying to make, but I know what the Spirit was doing in my heart. As she spoke, I sensed a deep longing. I thought, *I could do that. I want to do what she's doing!*

I didn't tell anyone. It was like a seed that I tucked into the place where dreams are planted. I kept it safe and protected. To tell someone would have exposed my tender dream to the trampling effect of a challenge or critique.

That seed of longing never went away. Eventually it began putting down roots and popped its head above ground. Little by little, what began as a secret hope has turned into a reality. Last month I had the pleasure of speaking at two women's retreats. My calendar for the coming year keeps filling with more, and I pray this trend will continue.

However, as you may have discovered, just because you *want* to be a speaker or writer, it doesn't mean you'll *get* to. That's where open doors come in.

OPEN DOORS

My first speaking engagement was with my mom at our church's moms group. Though we were both passionate about our topic, we felt exactly the opposite about speaking. She was dreading it, and I couldn't *wait!* When we walked into that room of about thirty moms, I was barely able to contain my excitement. My mom was barely able to contain her apprehension.

On our way out that day, the leader of the group said to me, "Shannon, that was good. *Really* good. You should think about getting that message published in a magazine!"

It was the first time I had ever considered being published. This was back before blogging, and I always considered writing something "professionals" did. But after hearing this suggestion, I liked it very much. That leader's brief compliment was enough to encourage me to try.

My writing time grew from Sunday afternoon naptime to weekday naptimes, too. I wrote and wrote, and after a month, I sent my first draft to the only writer I knew—my friend, Miriam. She graciously said, "It's good, but you might want to trim it down a bit." This was an understatement. My article was 5,000 words!

I spent another month trimming, then sent my little seedling article to the only two places I could think of—*Focus on the Family*, and my friend, Del Fehsenfeld, an editor at Life Action Ministries. To my great delight, they *both* wanted it.

I hadn't realized that simultaneous submissions were not advised (for this very reason), so I scrambled to revise my message into a second article. Amazingly, they both went to print.

The week that my article went out to the 1.5 million subscribers of *Focus on the Family Magazine,* I received several phone calls (this was before social media) from people who enjoyed my message. One southern woman left a message on the answering machine, saying, "Shay-annon, what you wrote, was just bee-autiful…." I kept her message on my machine for a year.

I was hooked. I loved writing! I loved the craft of shaping a message. I loved the honing. And I especially loved inspiring readers. And now, I not only wanted to be a speaker; I wanted to be a writer, too. God was clearly opening doors for me to begin.

YOUR TURN

Now that you've read my "foreword," I'd like you to think about your own. Pull out a journal or sheet of paper and write your response to these prompts:

1. **What stirred you to share your message?** When did *you* first have that burning desire to share something that would help or encourage others? What experiences prompted you to step out in faith?

2. **Who affirmed you?** Encouragement is so powerful. It can shape the way we see ourselves and our gifts. Who has encouraged you? Who affirmed your giftings? Who saw something in you that perhaps you didn't even see in yourself?

3. **What doors did God swing open?** What opportunities did you first have to use your gifts? What needs were you able to meet? Did God strategically put you in a group or location where your gifts were needed? How did God open those first doors that led to future opportunities?

Okay, now that you have your foreword written, I want you to add something right at the end. I want you to add the name of your foreword's author.

Don't be hasty. Stop and think for a moment. Who wrote this foreword? Who stirred your heart to share this message? Who surrounded you with people to encourage you and spur you on? Who swung those doors open for you?

Was it not God?

THE AUTHOR OF ALL

For each of us, the author of our foreword is God. He created us. We are His "handiwork." Any gifts or aptitudes we possess are from Him. We each reflect our Maker in unique ways. We each have unique callings. God *has* written your name beside specific assignments—each of which relate to His overarching purpose for all that He has created.

God is the Author of all, and He created this world to tell the story of Himself. And here's a jaw-dropping reality: God writes us in to His story! Yes, the story is all about Him, but we get to play a part. We each have roles. We each move the story forward, millimeter by millimeter. We don't have access to the Table of Contents because only God can see into the future. But we do have access to the "foreword."

We can look back and see our own "character development." We can see how God has been shaping and preparing us all along for our uniquely crafted assignments.

ONE BIG STORY

Think of various Bible characters and the assignments God gave them, which were prefaced with a "foreword":

- Moses was a Jewish boy, adopted by an Egyptian princess, who murdered a man and then spent forty years in the wilderness contemplating it all. This was his "foreword" before becoming the humble leader of God's people. (Exodus 2-3)

- Daniel was a Jewish teenager, born to nobility and abducted then trained in a Babylonian palace, who found creative ways to not defile himself and stay loyal to God. This was his "foreword" before becoming the trusted government administrator who influenced the king to decree that everyone fear and reverence God. (Daniel 1, 6)

- Mary was a devout Jewish virgin from Nazareth who became pregnant before sleeping with her fiancé Joseph, and who traveled with him to Bethlehem for a census just before her baby was born. This was her "foreword" before becoming the mother of Jesus and fulfilling the prophecies about the Messiah being born to a virgin in Bethlehem. (Isaiah 7:14, Micah 5:2, Luke 1-2)

- Paul was a devout Jewish Pharisee who grew up in a Greek town, a Roman citizen, and distinguished law student of Gamaliel whose zeal was focused on murdering Christians.[5] This was his "foreword" before being converted on the Damascus road, then traveling as a church planting missionary to both Jews and Greeks. (Acts 9)

These great men and women were part of the same story that you and I are part of. Our lives are being authored by the same God. The unique experiences that shape our pasts are all part of the "foreword" that God writes as a preface to the little part we each play in His overarching story.

TWO GROUPS OF INFLUENCERS

We've spent this chapter mostly in reflection. As encouraging as I hope it's been to consider God's hand in your past leading you to this point in your ministry, I think you'll find your "foreword" even more helpful for contemplating your future.

Take a moment and picture each of the people reading this book saying in unison, "God wrote my foreword. He set me up with this pen in my hand." (Or if you're more of a speaker, maybe it's a microphone in your hand.) But now, picture the readers in two groups: the overconfident and underconfident influencers.

We talked about this distinction in the first chapter, and I'm hoping you know which group you belong in. Let's consider how knowing your foreword can be uniquely helpful to each group.

The Foreword of the Underconfident

Are you someone who struggles with confidence? Do you feel nauseous when you think about sharing your new book on social media, wondering if people will think you're arrogant and full of yourself? Do you cringe every time you call yourself a writer or a speaker? Do you constantly obsess over trying to sound more humble?

If so, here's how your foreword can help. When you would rather go lock yourself in a closet until your book launch is over or cancel all of your upcoming speaking engagements, do this instead. Go back and re-read the foreword you just wrote in your journal. Remind yourself of the ways that God gave you this message. Review the ways other Christians have affirmed your gifts, and how God has used you in the past. Look back at all the doors God has opened for you. Now, step through them!

God has not given you a spirit of fear. He has given you a spirit of power—the power of His Spirit, which makes your ministry effective. He has given you a spirit of love—not love of yourself but a selfless love for others. And He has given you a spirit of self-control—the staying power that keeps you from running away from opportunities and enables you to embrace them instead (2 Timothy 1:7).

The Foreword of the Overconfident

Are you someone who has no trouble promoting your work? Do you easily step out with confidence? Do you make the mistake of relying on yourself and trusting in your own talent rather than purposefully depending on God? Do you often sound more humble than you truly are?

If so, here's how your foreword can help. When you'd be happy to dominate a conversation by sharing all of the success and growth your ministry has had, or you're tempted to call every church in North America and let them know about the ways you alone can transform their ministry, do this instead: Go back and re-read the foreword you just recorded in your journal.

Remind yourself that God gave you this message. Apart from Him you can do nothing, and every bit of truth you have to share originated from Him. He is the one who gave you any aptitude, gift, or training you've been privileged to receive. He has opened every single door that you've walked through.

No matter how comfortable or uncomfortable we are with spreading the truth of Jesus, our messages are each about Him. As Romans 11:36 says, "For from him and through him and to him are all things. To him be glory forever. Amen."

Won't you bow your head right now and thank God for your foreword, which provides the context for your ministry?

{CHAPTER FIVE}

STRATEGY

"How far that little candle throws his beams!
So shines a good deed in a weary world."
— *William Shakespeare*

I (Shannon) have had exactly one post go viral.

Actually, it wasn't even a blog post. It was a magazine article, published during the pre-social media, "email forwarding" era. Remember those days?

A few weeks after the story went to print, I was surprised when friends began calling, emailing, or stopping me in the grocery store to say, "Someone forwarded me a story you wrote! The one about your little boy in the bathroom stall? Oh, I laughed till I cried!"

Yes, it was bathroom humor widening my reach with each forwarded email, but I didn't mind. I proudly owned my new identity as the Costco mom whose little boy had said, "Uh oh, Mommy... Doze stinkies are making me frow up!"

I knew my story had truly gone viral the day a Costco employee scanned my card, then looked up in surprise and said, "Oh! I read your story! Did that happen in *our* store?"

"Uh… yes sir, it did."

"Potty Talk" was reposted and passed around for months. One woman began taping copies up in public rest rooms around her town. The article won first place for "Humorous Article" at the Evangelical Press Association. Then a media company contracted with me to create an animated video based on the story. I even had an acquisition editor, whose wife had sent him the article, call me about writing a book!

I was beyond delighted with my laughter-spreading success, and was dreaming of where it would all lead. I could already see my name in bylines. And in headlines. And at the end of shopping lines, with people pressing forward to buy my latest hilarious book.

But alas, none of that happened. Slowly, the laughter died out. The video didn't sell many copies. And the acquisition editor never responded, even after I scrambled to pull together a book proposal. I went on to write other equally funny stories, but even the ones that got published didn't catch fire like that first one. My tenure as a viral writer quietly expired.

HOW RANDOM IS SUCCESS?

Does publishing success ever seem rather random to you? Honestly, I've seen messages I didn't think were outstanding reach millions. I've seen other unequivocally stellar messages that never make it off the ground—even with marketing gurus in the background giving it their best shot.

Why is that? And what role does God play? Does He wave His sovereign wand of blessing over particular messages or messengers to create certain windfall? If so, does He employ a formula for choosing?

Equally important, how should I respond to these mysteries? Should I keep looking for strategic ways to grow my reach? Should I work on growing my Twitter followers? Should I pay to boost my posts on Facebook? Should I target particular audiences? Or should I ditch all efforts to publicize my work and swivel my attention-gathering efforts toward God?

When our hearts are either obsessing over tactics and strategies or chafing against God for not granting us success; when all of our efforts are couched in a desire to go "viral," there's a good chance we've drifted from our purpose. We've once again become fixated on attracting followers for ourselves, not God. We're focused on lifting ourselves up, not Christ.

Am I suggesting that as Christian influencers, we must become strategy-free purists? That we should abandon all campaign-building, goal-setting, and marketing-driven efforts? Not at all. I'm simply suggesting that we should focus on the goals that Jesus commissioned us with, and use strategy the way He taught us to.

So *was* Jesus strategic? I'm convinced He was. In fact, let me invite you to join a private conversation between Jesus and His disciples, in which He taught two strategies for spreading truth and light that still provide clarity for us today.

SCATTERING SEED

In Luke 8:4-8, Jesus told what most Bibles call the "Parable of the Sower." But the sower isn't really the main character. The story opens with the sower scattering seed (the Word of God), but there is no emphasis on his skill, strategy, or focus. Instead, he seems to scatter seed indiscriminately, letting it fall where it will.

This is a good picture of us, as influencers for the kingdom of God. We reach into our supply of truth and toss out seeds by the fistful. But even when we employ publicity strategies and pay for marketing campaigns, we can't ultimately determine how our audience will respond. Sure, improved skill and increased marketing dollars often translate into louder applause, heightened buzz, clicked links, and more book sales. But for all of our efforts, we cannot capture the most important result. We cannot cause seeds to take root in receptive hearts.

Just like in Jesus' story, some of our words bounce against cemented hearts. Other truths may sink in shallowly for a moment, then quickly wither. Even when our words do become rooted deeply, creating heart change and the fruit that goes with it, we must admit that this is not our doing. We must rejoice in the miraculous work of God!

After Jesus told this parable, His disciples huddled up and said, "Can you explain, please?" (Luke 8:9-15) Here are the men who will soon be the primary sowers of the gospel. But as Jesus explains the parable, he doesn't offer even one strategy for seed tossing. This is remarkable! In a moment, we'll turn our attention to the strategy Jesus *does* offer His disciples, but stop for a moment and consider what this means for your own ministry.

Each of us, as influencers for the gospel, would love to see our messages multiply into orchards loaded with spiritual fruit. Who doesn't want to be the sower whose seed "fell into good soil and grew and yielded a hundredfold"? (Luke 8:8) I would love nothing more, and I'm guessing you feel the same.

Yet, the results of our truth-sharing ministries lie ultimately in God's hands, not ours.

LAYING DOWN MY BURDEN

In my book, *Control Girl,* I shared repeatedly about God being in control—and how that's *good news* for us. Both as men and women, control is a burden that we tend to heap onto our own shoulders. Yet, as we convince ourselves that we should and must manage all of the contingencies and make everything turn out "right," we only become stressed out, anxious, and angry. Why? Because we're not ultimately in control. God is.

Now, I tend to have no problem *saying* that God is in control. I'm happy to sing out "I surrender all" and "Jesus take the wheel," but then without even noting the discrepancy, I turn on my heel and pick up my burden of control. As an influencer, when I grip my seed bag tightly, convincing myself that it's all up to me to get truth into hearts, the results are never positive.

I become...

- Anxious over the future of publishing, our culture, and our nation

- Worried about what people thought when they heard me speak or when they read what I wrote

- Angry over bottlenecks, rejections, and harsh critiques

- Stressed, wondering if I'll ever finish on time

- Perfectionistic, driving myself to exhaustion

Friend, take it from someone who has tried to lunge for control in hundreds, maybe thousands of ways. Getting and having and keeping control can't be done. And when I try, I only make myself (and often others) miserable.

Thankfully, God never asked me to take control. In fact, He doesn't *want* me trying to take control. He wants me to trust Him. He's already in control, so I don't have to be. Reminding myself of this brings the peace, security, and joy that control never will.

STRATEGY #1: LISTEN WELL

Jesus explains the parable of the sower to His disciples, then concludes by saying, "Take care, then, how you hear" (Luke 8:18).

Wait. Take care how they *hear*? Wouldn't it be more important for Jesus to give these influencers—the very ones who will soon kick off the Jesus movement, spreading truth about Him to the entire world—instruction on how to *speak*?

Nope. Even for these very first seed tossers of the gospel, Jesus' emphasis is on *hearing* well, not spreading well. And it's the same for us. If Jesus were to pull a modern group of influencers together—you and me, included—for a consultation on how to spread truth most effectively in our day, I think He would encourage us to stop obsessing over how to attract and acquire more followers. I think He would give us the same advice that He gave His disciples: "Take care, then, how you hear" (Luke 8:18).

For all who take up the mantle of spreading truth, our first responsibility is to hear well, for without receiving we have nothing to give. Whether we're in church, engaged in a small group discussion, spending time alone with God, or reading other Christians' work, we must discern and welcome the truth with "ears that hear," as Jesus puts it. This is our main role, and it's something we *do* have control over.

Incidentally, as we listen to the Spirit of God, we become more consumed with Jesus and less consumed with ourselves. If we feel burdened by the pressure to sell ourselves and our work, we're not listening. If we're wringing our hands, obsessed that someone has misrepresented us, we're not listening. And if we're consumed with efforts to go viral, we're certainly not listening. We've once again become distracted by the noise of the world.

SHARING SECRETS

On the other hand, if we've received a heaping dose of helpful truth from God's Word, we should be bursting to share it! This is the natural result of hearing well.

I'm guessing this is exactly how the disciples felt after their private parable-explanation session with the Lord. Jesus used parables to *hide* truth from certain people in the crowd—most likely the Pharisees who would one day kill Him (Luke 8:11). But Jesus said, "To you it has been given to know the secrets of the kingdom." They were in on something big!

Soon, these men would be taking the whispered secrets of Jesus and shouting them from the housetops (Matthew 10:27, Luke 8:17). But first, it was important for the disciples—the ones to whom Jesus was entrusting the secrets—to "take care how they heard" (Luke 8:18).

As modern disciples, entrusted with the secrets of the kingdom, we also need to lean in and listen carefully to our Lord. But then what?

If we have listened well and have a burning message to share, is there ever a time that we should pursue a publisher? Should we consider self-publication? Should we bother using slides while speaking, and labor over the transitions from one point to the next? Should we tweet out quotes and special sale prices once a book is in print? Should we post Instagram photos of ourselves standing behind a microphone, hoping to trigger more speaking opportunities?

STRATEGY #2: STEP ONTO YOUR PLATFORM

I imagine the disciples had similar questions. Not about slides or Instagram, of course, but when you're entrusted with something this important, you naturally want to understand how to use it. What were they to *do* with the truth they had received?

Whether or not the disciples asked these questions out loud, Jesus provided an answer. Sandwiched between His explanation of the parable of the sower and His exhortation to listen well, Jesus offers His disciples a second strategy:

> "No one after lighting a lamp covers it with a jar or puts it under a bed, but puts it on a stand, so that those who enter may see the light" (Luke 8:16).

I've studied this verse before, but I always plucked it out of context instead of reading it as part of Jesus' unpacking of the Parable of the Sower. Yet it's smack dab in the middle of the conversation, so it only makes sense to consider these two images of the soil and the lamp together.

The "good soil" represents the person who has gladly received God's Word. Similarly, the lit lamp represents someone whose eyes have been opened to truth.

A LIT LAMP

Picture "this present darkness" into which each of us has been born (Ephesians 6:12). We all begin life with our minds blinded to truth so that we do not immediately see the light of the gospel of the glory of Christ (2 Corinthians 4:4). But then, some of us experience a miracle! The lamp of our understanding is lit, and we see the worth and glory and desirableness of Jesus.

This is what the disciples (minus Judas) experienced. They miraculously saw Jesus as the One worthy of leaving everything to follow. And now it's slowly dawning on them that He is the Son of God who has come to take away the sins of the world.

Using this metaphor of the lit lamp, Jesus states the obvious. You wouldn't cover a lamp with a jar, since the lack of oxygen would snuff it out. You wouldn't put it under a bed because it would have no purpose there (plus, your bed might catch fire!). Instead, you put it on a stand. You lift up that lamp so that its light can spread for others to see.

But, consider this. Who lights the lamp? Who brings understanding to our darkened hearts and minds? Is it not the Spirit of God who gives us eyes to see and ears to hear? When Jesus says, "No one after lighting a lamp...", He's inviting us to consider the strategy *God* employs.

God is the One who lights the lamp, and God is the One who sets it on a stand. He doesn't tuck it away where no one would see it. No, God is strategic! He lights up our understanding and then sets us on a stand. A platform.

And what is God's strategic end goal? Is He calling attention to the lamp? Does He intend for people to gather around and admire its brightness? No, He wants others to be drawn to the light, that the light might spread.

The disciples would soon be placed on lampstands far and wide to share about the "Light of the world" (John 8:12). This was God's light-spreading strategy. As light receivers, they were asked to simply stand on whatever platform God had placed beneath their feet and shine! For Peter, this involved preaching. For Matthew and John, it involved writing. What will it entail for you?

God has strategically placed you right where you are for a reason. He has blessed you with unique giftings and a custom-made sphere of influence, and now He's calling you to shine! To smear the darkness with light! To boldly step out onto your platform and offer contrast to a darkened world.

When others see the light and are drawn to God, it won't be because you have learned the correct tactic for shedding light or because you will have targeted the perfect patch of darkness. No, your role is to simply step onto the platform God has given you and to share the light, or understanding, which you have received.

Like the "good soil," we receive truth. Then like strategically placed lamps, we spread it.[6]

SPREADING LIGHT

Today—as I am writing this—a designer is working on my website. This is the first money in ten years that I have ever spent on my site. I've always taught myself how to do whatever is needed, but lately I've been so busy with the speaking and writing assignments God has given me that my website has gone untended. So I hired another Christian woman who is passionate about using website design to spread light into the darkness.

The result, I trust, will be a cleaner, prettier, faster, more intuitive site which will serve people well. My hope is for my blog to toss out seeds of truth, hope, and joy. I want to step onto my little platform as a recent first-time author and do whatever I can to spread light.

Will more people be drawn to my site? Will my Google rankings improve? Will visitors stay longer and click more because of the fast response and slick design? And what about spiritual fruit? Will people who live in brokenness and pain be attracted to the light? Will my tossed seeds take root in hearts? Will any fruit sprout and grow?

Oh, how I hope so! I long to be used by God in these ways. I'm excited to listen well, and use my updated site to scatter the truth I have received even farther. But the multiplication process is not up to me. And this is good news, remember? For what if my effectiveness as a speaker and writer was contingent on my own skill or dedication? What if God was depending on me to provide a state-of-the-art website? That is a burden I'm so glad I don't have to carry.

Yet my work is not void of strategy. God has lit the lamp of my understanding and strategically placed me on a platform to spread light. What joy that I get to be part of His work!

OUR STRATEGIC WORK

Friends, our God is strategic! And we are called to be strategic, too. For me, that means investing in an updated website. For you, it might mean going to a conference, taking a class, reaching out to an agent, or buying some new equipment.

As a result, our work might go viral...or it might not. Regardless, here's what we must remember: Since God is ultimately in control of the results, we shouldn't be wringing our hands, worried about what people think, or obsessing over statistics and where it's all headed. Instead, our role is simple. We get to be lamps, lit with understanding. We get to step onto our platforms, strategically shine, then leave the multiplying results up to God.

{CHAPTER SIX}

PRIDE

*"God sends no one away empty except those
who are full of themselves."*
– *D.L. Moody*

When my (Kate) kids were young, we sometimes listened to Disney songs in the car. One morning while listening to "Part of Your World" from The Little Mermaid soundtrack, my kids and I heard Ariel sing about how she had plenty of gadgets and gizmos, and more than enough "thingama-bobs" than she could ever need. She boasted about being the girl who had everything, and yet she wanted more.

Suddenly my three-year-old daughter gasped, "Mom! She's being *proud!*"

She spat out the word "proud" like it was a contagious disease. First I was amused that she picked up on such a subtle nuance in the song. Then my own pride followed quickly on the heels of my amusement: *Gosh, I am such a good parent! Look at that… My three-year-old can spot the sin of pride in a song without even being prompted! I have taught her so well.*

Perhaps my daughter was right to treat pride like a contagious disease—isn't that exactly what it is? We "caught" it from Adam and Eve, who wanted to "be like God" (Genesis 3:5-6)—and ever since then, the pandemic continues to be passed on from person to person and generation to generation. From the very beginning, humankind has been on a quest to be like God. To be exalted and elevated. To know and be known.

Now, even a toddler can spot the gaudy appearance of pride from the back seat of a car. It reminds me of the song, "Shiny," from the 2016 Disney movie, Moana. In the catchy tune, a corrupt crab named Tamatoa belts out lyrics about how glamorous he has made himself by adding glitzy jewels and other sparkly trinkets to his shell. To onlookers he's obviously gaudy, yet he keeps strutting his stuff for all to admire. Isn't that the way pride works?

In our sinful, selfish, post-Eden phase, we can't get enough praise. Like Ariel from The Little Mermaid and Tamatoa from Moana, we want more.

THE INSATIABLE NATURE OF PRAISE

If we're honest with ourselves and with God, most of us would confess that we like positive attention. Even if you're the type of person who *hates* the spotlight, I'm guessing you would still agree that deep down it feels nice to be *known*. Don't the edges of our lips curl up into a smile when someone notices one of our accomplishments or compliments something we've done? It took me a long time to admit, but I see it in myself: I crave verbal affirmation.

But here's the thing: Even though it sure feels nice in the moment, praise never fully satisfies. It always leaves us hungry for more. John Piper points out that praise from others "is like a drug. It gives a buzz and then it is gone.

You have got to have another fix. You are always insecure. You are always needy of other people's praise in order for you to be happy or to feel secure. You are never satisfied."[7] As the character Jenny Lind sings in the 2017 film, The Greatest Showman, a thousand spotlights—even the whole world—will never be enough.

In a Desiring God article, guest writer Mike Schumann uses Madonna as an example. "After selling *one hundred million* albums worldwide, she says, 'Even though I've become somebody, I still have to prove that somebody. My struggle has never ended and it probably never will.' In other words, she has climbed to the top of the tower and all it has given her in return is a temporary satisfaction followed by a greater sense of emptiness and burden than ever before. Fame, no matter the quantity, fails to satisfy the soul."[8]

Yet as believers in Christ, we know One who satisfies the soul not only in this life, but for all eternity. "Then Jesus declared, 'I am the bread of life. Whoever comes to me will never go hungry, and whoever believes in me will never be thirsty'" (John 6:35, NIV). He alone can satisfy us—and He alone is worthy of all glory and praise. "You are worthy, our Lord and God, to receive glory and honor and power, for you created all things, and by your will they were created and have their being" (Revelation 4:11, NIV).

We know these truths in our minds and agree with our lips, but do we truly believe them in our hearts and display them with our lives?

THE SELFIE GENERATION

In 2013, Oxford Dictionaries announced "selfie" as the International Word of the Year.[9] Apparently its frequency in the English language increased by 17,000% since the previous year.[10] Talk about a trend revealing of its culture.

Speaker and author Adriel Booker points out, "While

I believe it's important to both create and make space for beauty, this Instagram-centric world is only helping us see what was already there in the first place: we are obsessed with ourselves and infatuated with the idea of being important and admired."

Those who profess faith in Christ are not immune to this temptation or obsession. It's so easy to become the life jacket *model* instead of the life jacket *distributor*. Amongst both Christians and unbelievers in this "selfie" generation, "Look at me!" is far more common than "Look to Him!"

Adriel compares our tendencies with the example of Christ: "Jesus trusted the work of the Father in people's hearts and always pointed to Him, not Himself. Too many platform builders are so concerned about building their brand that they are making their own image an idol. None of us are exempt from this pull."

She goes on with this encouragement to Christian writers, speakers, and influencers: "Let's focus on serving our readers and listeners and pointing them to Jesus. As we do, others *will* invite their friends because Jesus—when we see Him in all His goodness—is incredibly hard not to fall in love with. Let's not forget how attractive and amazing He really is."

Great advice, isn't it? And if we do what Adriel suggests and remember just how attractive and amazing God really is, another outcome will naturally occur—our pride will dissipate as we're humbled by our own condition in comparison to His perfection and holiness.

BUILDING KINGDOMS

We know from Scripture that God is not pleased with those who try to exalt themselves. In fact, He takes pride incredibly seriously. It's not just a "light, respectable sin," as if there were such a thing. In the fourth chapter of Daniel, we read that King Nebuchadnezzar had grown and become strong. His greatness was described as reaching to heaven, and his dominion as spanning to the ends of the earth (Daniel 4:22). Perhaps this is the way we'd describe the platforms and social media followings of certain powerhouse Christian influencers. Maybe we even wish for that kind of reach ourselves. But as Luke 12:48 says, "From everyone who has been given much, much will be demanded; and from the one who has been entrusted with much, much more will be asked" (NIV).

One day when Nebuchadnezzar "was walking on the roof of the royal palace of Babylon, the king said, 'Is not this great Babylon, which I have built by my mighty power as a royal residence and for the glory of my majesty?'" (Daniel 4:30) Notice the king's emphasis. He attributes his earthly success to his own power and openly admits that he created it for his own glory. This is a pretty arrogant viewpoint, don't you think? Yet many Christian influencers secretly have the same view of their "success."

God doesn't let Nebuchadnezzar's haughty attitude last for long. In fact, "while the words were still in the king's mouth, there fell a voice from heaven, 'O King Nebuchadnezzar, to you it is spoken: The kingdom has departed from you, and you shall be driven from among men, and your dwelling shall be with the beasts of the field. And you shall be made to eat grass like an ox, and seven periods of time shall pass over you, until you know that the Most High rules the kingdom of men and gives it to whom he will.' Immediately the word was fulfilled against Nebuchadnezzar. He was driven from among men and ate grass like an ox, and his body was wet with the dew of heaven till his hair grew as long as eagles' feathers, and his nails were like birds' claws" (Daniel 4:31-33). Scary, isn't it? Who's to say that God won't do the same to any of us who secretly (or openly) believe our fame or popularity are the result of our own doing?

At the end of the Lord's allotted time for Nebuchadnezzar's punishment, God graciously restored the king's reason and his kingdom. Then the king proclaimed, "Now I, Nebuchadnezzar, praise and extol and honor the King of heaven, for all his works are right and his ways are just; and *those who walk in pride he is able to humble*" (Daniel 4:37, italics mine). Nebuchadnezzar had to learn his lesson the hard way. May God be gracious to help us heed the warning from his example, and squash any hint of pride we see appearing in our hearts.

BUILDING TOWERS

God gives us another poignant example in Genesis 11, with the story of the Tower of Babel. The people of that time said, "Come, let us build ourselves a city and a tower with its top in the heavens, and let us make a name for ourselves, lest we be dispersed over the face of the whole earth" (Genesis 11:4). Did you catch that? *Let us make a name for ourselves.* Isn't that exactly what we're doing when we attempt to build a platform? Aren't we trying to make a name for ourselves? How are we any different?

Here's the scary part: Guess what God did to the tower builders in Genesis 11? *He frustrated their language.* He confused their speech (Genesis 11:7). He limited their source of communication.

With a reverent and holy fear, I should stand back and recognize that God could very well do the same thing to me. If my writing is motivated by pride or a desire to promote myself, God would do well to frustrate and confuse my language. He would be wise and right to limit my reach, remove my audience, and cut off my means of communication.

Whether I'm seeking to build a kingdom, a tower, or a platform—"unless the Lord builds the house, those who build it labor in vain" (Psalm 127:1). When I go my own way and try to take matters into my own hands, nothing good comes of it. In fact, I quickly slide down the sand dune into selfish ambition.

BUILDING ON SAND

Growing up on the shores of Lake Michigan, the beach was both my playground and my sanctuary. I spent my childhood summers splashing in the unsalted waves, playing tag, and having underwater handstand competitions with my sister. We sprawled out on our beach towels with books and potato chips, inevitably crunching grains of sand between our teeth.

Every once in a while we parked ourselves at the edge of the lake, determined to craft a masterpiece where the waves lapped at the shore. We crouched in our damp bathing suits for hours on end, sculpting and shaping, digging and patting the wet sand into our grand vision. We built castles and towers with curved moats to deter any threatening water from damaging our works of art.

Once we deemed the creation complete, we called to our mom, who was either napping in her beach chair or lost in a Rosamunde Pilcher novel. "Come look at what we made!" She stirred back to reality and came to gush about our latest efforts. "Oh wow! Look at that! I'm so impressed!" She knew just how to make us feel good. I let her words of praise sink in, my pride sparkling from my toothy smile.

Looking back, I'm not sure what delusion I was under. Perhaps it was called naiveté—or childhood. But without fail, I assumed that our sand masterpiece would exist forever. Maybe I thought it would morph into a concrete monument, a permanent fixture for all passing by to admire.

Jesus knew people like me during His time on earth. He talked about it in His famous Sermon on the Mount: "Beware of practicing your righteousness before other people in order to be seen by them, for then you will have no reward from your Father who is in heaven" (Matthew 6:1). Jesus goes on to list a number of scenarios based on the lives of the Pharisees—giving to the needy, praying, fasting. In each example, He warns His listeners not to be like the hypocrites, who do what they do in public to be seen and praised by others (Matthew 6:2, 5, 16).

Author Kyle Idleman says that the best definition he knows of the "Pharisee life" is this: "Everything they do is done for other people to see."[11] I bet if the Pharisees had built a sand castle, they would have placed it in a strategically prominent place for all to admire. But wait a second. Any time I post something online, am I not doing it in order to be seen by others? Isn't that the whole point?

In every single one of those examples from His Sermon on the Mount, Jesus finishes by saying, "Truly, I say to you, they have received their reward" (Matthew 6:2, 5, 16). In other words, they got what they wanted. They sought the praise of men, and they received it—and that's all they would get. Period.

Instead of giving, praying, or fasting like the Pharisees, Jesus instructs His followers to do those things secretly to be seen by their Father in heaven, who will surely reward them (Matthew 6:4, 6, 18). Which would you rather have—a temporary reward of praise from the world, or a lasting reward from your Father in heaven?

Jesus doesn't stop there. He goes on to teach, "Do not lay up for yourselves treasures on earth, where moth and rust destroy and where thieves break in and steal, but lay up for yourselves treasures in heaven, where neither moth nor rust destroys and where thieves do not break in and steal. For where your treasure is, there your heart will be also" (Matthew 6:19-21).

If we ask the Lord to dig for the buried treasure in our hearts, what would He find? Where is your treasure stored?

Does it lie in the number of Twitter followers or blog subscribers you have? Can it be found in the number of likes and comments you get on Facebook?

Maybe I'm wrong, but don't most aspects of platform building fall into the category of "treasures on earth"? After all, we can't take any of the stats, recognition, or online profiles with us to heaven. This is why it's so critical that we see each "number"—each Instagram follower, email subscriber, or website click—for what they really are: a person made in the image of God with an eternal soul. From this perspective, our influence and efforts *can* have a lasting impact, with God's help. But we should never weigh our sense of identity by the size of our following.

Like my prized childhood sandcastle, our online identities won't last forever. Inevitably, before the sun slipped into the water at the end of my beach day, a renegade wave would tumble over my hand-built tower. If I was still there to see it, I would gasp and groan and act like the world had ended. "Oh No! It's *ruined*! All my hard *work*!" With a single wave, my efforts and pride washed away.

One day we will die, and all of our social media accounts, websites, and speaking schedules will get swept into the sea. Even before that, it's entirely possible that one day we'll wake up and discover that our Twitter account has been hacked, our website has been compromised, our identity has been stolen. With a single crash, we could lose it all. The only grains left will be those with eternal significance—namely, any spiritual impact that our work for the Lord has had on readers and listeners.

With this in mind, let's remember: If our entire sense of identity and purpose is built on the size of our following or dependent on the praise and admiration of others, we're building on sand.

ANONYMOUS ART

During a recent visit to the beach near our house, my family and I came upon the most magnificent sandcastle I've ever seen in my life. It was taller than me, and incredibly ornate and detailed on every side. Clearly the sculptors had professional tools and spent hours crafting the jaw-dropping masterpiece.

Onlookers gathered around to admire the work, turning to strangers nearby: "Did you do this?" One by one, each person standing on the shoreline shook their head.

The artists were nowhere to be found. They had labored in the sun and heat to create a remarkable work of art, then just walked away, without a clue or trace as to their identity. No name or signature could be seen anywhere near the sculpture. Except for those present during its creation, nobody knew who made it.

These Mystery Sandcastle Masters were the opposite of the Pharisees. They were content to do the best work they could do and walk away, leaving their creation for others to enjoy without their knowledge.

WHO ARE YOU?

The sandcastle sculptors could walk away from their work unidentified, but much of the writing and speaking life doesn't work that way, does it? Especially if you're trying to grow the scope of your reach. Unless you decide to write anonymously, ghostwrite for another author, or use a pseudonym, we're often prompted to establish online identities for various reasons—some good, some not-so-good.

Whenever I'm prompted to type a personal bio into the short space allotted on one of my social media accounts, my pulse escalates. I feel the pressure to perform. My natural inclination is to include the best-sounding accolades and titles I can muster up. If I only get a limited number of characters, I better make a good impression, right?

I'm tempted to highlight things I've accomplished, positions I've held, and links to past work and achievements. Maybe if I sound impressive enough, people will follow me.

Unlike the Mystery Sandcastle Masters, deep down, I want to be *known*.

But by whom, exactly, and for what purpose?

One day as I was clicking around Twitter, I came across Lore Ferguson Wilbert's profile. I had heard her name in a few different places online, so I paused to read more about her. Her bio not only pleasantly surprised me, it also refreshed and convicted me. Unlike so many others (including myself), she had written simply, "Nothing to commend me except Christ, his life, death, and life again. On that rock alone I stand."[12]

Amen! Isn't that what all believers should proclaim?

In Galatians 6:14, Paul says, "But far be it from me to boast except in the cross of our Lord Jesus Christ, by which the world has been crucified to me, and I to the world." If I stop to think about it, I realize I have no reason to boast apart from anything tied to the Lord's work in my life.

If I have a biblical view of myself, I have to admit I am nothing without Him. I would still be dead in my sins—and last time I checked, dead people don't accomplish much worth boasting about. Anything good that I have or do comes directly from my Maker. Without Him, I don't even have breath in my lungs. Martin Luther offers this hopeful perspective: "God created the world out of nothing, and so long as we are nothing, He can make something out of us."

These stanzas from the hymn, "When I Survey the Wondrous Cross" come to mind:

When I survey the wondrous cross
On which the Prince of glory died,

My richest gain I count but loss,
And pour contempt on all my pride.

Forbid it, Lord, that I should boast,
Save in the death of Christ my God!
All the vain things that charm me most,
I sacrifice them to His blood.[13]

In those moments when I'm tempted to perform or make a good impression, when I'm distracted by "all the vain things that charm me most," may God help me to survey the wondrous cross, to pour contempt on all my pride, to count my gains as loss, and to boast only in the death of Christ. May He teach me to sculpt the best sandcastle I can with His help, then walk away.

In Him I'm already known more intimately than I can fathom by the One who knit me together in my mother's womb. The same One who knows every star in the sky also knows every hair on my head. Is it not enough to be known and loved by Him? Who else's attention am I seeking, if I already have His?

FOLLOWING IN HIS FOOTSTEPS

If we seek to be Christ-following influencers, we would do well to follow His example in every way, including His demonstration of leadership.

Let's take Jesus' triumphal entry into Jerusalem, for example (Matthew 21:1-11, Mark 11:1-10, Luke 19:28-40, John 12:12-15). The people at the time were waiting for a King, a Messiah. Some even believed that Jesus was the One—the One who would rescue them from the heavy Roman oppression.

And they were right—but He didn't come or act in the way that anyone expected. He had every right to organize a huge parade in His honor, complete with chariots and regal horses. He could have been decked out in royal robes as He made His way to His rightful place as King—to sit on the throne in the palace.

But instead of an ornate chariot, He sat on a borrowed colt. Instead of wearing expensive robes, He sat on a pile of cloaks that other people hastily draped over the animal's back. And instead of going to the palace, He went to the temple—to His Father's house.

We could go on and on about Jesus' "upside-down" kingdom. Even His initial entry into this world didn't happen with fanfare or trumpets sounding—He entered through a humble maidservant's womb, born in a stable.

Though He is King of the universe, instead of a golden crown, He wore a crown of thorns. Instead of accepting the praise of men, He accepted their ridicule, scorn, and ultimately the full weight and punishment of their sin.

If this is the example we are to follow, who are we to elevate ourselves or our own name? James 4:10 instructs, "Humble yourselves before the Lord, and he will exalt you." It's God's prerogative to exalt, not our own. St. Augustine echoes, "Do you wish to rise? You plan a tower that will pierce the clouds. Lay first the Foundation of Humility."

Philippians 2 spells it out for us plainly:

"Do nothing out of selfish ambition or conceit, but in humility count others more significant than yourselves. Let each of you look not only to his own interests, but also to the interests of others. Have this mind among yourselves, which is yours in Christ Jesus, who, though he was in the form of God, did not count equality with God a thing to be grasped, but emptied himself, by taking the form of a servant, being born in the likeness of men. And being found in human form, he humbled himself by becoming obedient to the point of death, even death on a cross." (Philippians 2:3-8)

Have this mind among yourselves. This is our example. This is who we are to imitate.

We could look at Jesus' example and be tempted to give up altogether. There's no way we could ever attain to His standard, so why even try? Or, we could look at His example and let it spur us on. In Hebrews 12:3, we read, "Consider him who endured from sinners such hostility against himself, *so that you may not grow weary or faint-hearted*" (italics mine). Hebrews 10:24 (NIV) says, ". . . let us consider how we may spur one another on to love and good deeds."

Instead of taking more selfies, let's flip the camera around and capture snapshots of God in action. Let's turn the lens on Him, not ourselves. With His help, let's boast in His work, not our own. Let's seek to build His eternal kingdom, not a temporary sand castle of fame. Let's elevate His name, not ours.

{CHAPTER SEVEN}

COMPARE

*"The moment you stop caring what other people
think most about you is most likely when you
start doing what God wants most."*

— *Ann Voskamp*

After my (Shannon) first book came out, my husband began regularly checking my Amazon rankings. He would call me in the middle of the day and say, "Honey, look! You're up to #15,542 today!" Who knew I'd ever consider 15,542nd place something to celebrate, but I did!

After one such phone call, I said, "Hey look up an author named Christy Smith" (not her real name). Christy's book had come out exactly the same time mine did, so I wondered how the two compared. "Mmmm…" I heard my husband's voice fall a bit. "Are you sure you want to know?" My heart sank when he told me.

The next day I decided to check Christy's Amazon rank on my own to see if her superior score was a fluke. Then

I checked the following day to see if it was a several-day-fluke. Comparing my rank against Christy's became a habit. Most times hers was higher than mine, but occasionally it was lower. My heart would soar with pride or deflate with jealousy accordingly—all in a moment's glance.

JUST STOP?

Comparing myself with other influencers is such a distraction from what God has called me to do. It is never productive. And while I've heard lots of people agree with this and say that we need to stop comparing, I rarely hear anyone giving instruction on how to do that.

I mean, there's the obvious suggestion to "just stop." But comparison is as intuitive as noticing that one author got an award and I didn't. I'm not sure we *can* stop comparing—especially in this new digital age, which offers exponential comparison tools for measuring everything from website traffic to social media "shares" to Google analytics.

So what should we do? Stop reading the data? Stop opening the results of our Facebook ads? Stop looking at our blog analytics?

In the situation with Christy's Amazon rank, I found that I *did* need to stop looking at the numbers. It was counterproductive, so I made a commitment to stop several months ago and haven't looked back since.

But you know what happened just last week? I opened my Instagram account and noticed another author whose first book also released around the same time as mine. She was sharing a photo of herself signing her next contract. I thought, *What? Another one! That's her third book now, and I'm only on my second!*

Then I thought, *Oh, no. I'm comparing again.*

ENEMY AT WORK

Friends, this is just what our enemy wants. Notice the connection between jealousy and Satan's agenda for us in these verses:

> "If your heart is one that bleeds dark streams of jealousy and selfishness, do not be so proud that you ignore your depraved state. The wisdom of this world should never be mistaken for heavenly wisdom; it originates below in the earthly realms, with the demons. Any place where you find jealousy and selfish ambition, you will discover chaos and evil thriving under its rule." (James 3:14-16, The Voice)

When we're jealous or obsessed with selfish ambition to get ahead, we are caving in to Satan's influence. Our enemy wants us to compare for two reasons: 1) comparison leads us into the bondage of either pride or worthlessness; and 2) comparison leads to isolation. Let me share a personal example of how this works.

Once when I arrived to speak at a women's event, another speaker arrived at the same time. There had been a scheduling error. To solve the problem, the leaders set up two rooms. The women were invited to head either to my room to hear a deeply spiritual talk about leaving everything to follow Jesus, or down the hall to hear about organizing their kitchens.

As you can imagine, there was a mass exodus down the hall. Before the meeting began, I pulled a friend aside and shared my discouragement. She said, "Shannon, don't worry about what's going on down there. Focus on the people who *did* choose to hear your message!"

What beautiful advice, right? I wish I had taken it.

As I stood before my little group, I was completely distracted. Why did everyone flock to the other speaker? Did the high attendance in that other room make a statement about me? Then I had a new thought. Perhaps the choice those women made to flock to the lighthearted topic room was an indictment against *them*. I almost felt sorry for their shallow souls!

After speaking that morning, I caught a glimpse of the other speaker coming down the hall. She was a woman I had always wanted to get to know, but instead of greeting her, I quickly darted into the bathroom. She was now on my list of people to avoid, not pursue.

COMPARISON'S TRAP

Do you see how I fell right into Satan's comparison trap? Our enemy loves to get us comparing, because he knows it will result in one of two outcomes—both of which create bondage. Either we compare and find that we are inferior, which leads to shame, jealousy, and insecurity. Or we compare and find that we are superior, which leads to pride, arrogance, and self-exaltation. In some instances (like the example I just shared) we fall into *both* traps. Either way, Satan wins. He not only burdens us with our own hang-ups, he also uses this to cause us to pull away from each other.

Notice how I darted into the bathroom, rather than connecting with the other speaker. And my new disdain for the women who attended the kitchen organizing workshop didn't exactly draw me closer to them. Comparison drives wedges into relationships. We pull away, rather than drawing near. And when does Satan have the greater advantage—when we're isolated, or when we're tightly packed into community relationships?

God, in His wisdom, designed us to be part of a team. Working collaboratively guards us against inferiority *and* superiority. As we discover our own unique gifts and appreciate the unique gifts of others, we become indispensable to each other. We are always stronger together. And we are always weaker alone.

So as we consider building platforms that lift Jesus high, we've got to be vigilant about doing so *together*. If we're going to truly embrace each other and link arms as teammates, we've got to root out whatever is causing us to be jealous or to gloat.

STRATEGIC SEATING

Luke 14 tells of the day Jesus dined in the home of a Pharisee ruler. Since the Jewish people practiced no separation of church and state, these Pharisees served as both the political and spiritual leaders of their day. Whether you went to church, the market, or court, these guys were in charge.

But even among the Pharisees, there was a pecking order. Jesus picked up on it when He noticed the way they seated themselves at the table. Apparently the seating arrangement offered a tangible way for mapping out the social hierarchy, with higher ranking seats and lower ranking ones—and these guys were all vying for the best seats.

I find it interesting that Jesus didn't respond by saying, "You all need to stop this comparing. It's a trap!" Instead, Jesus told them what they needed to *start* doing.

He began by painting a scenario. "You've been invited to a wedding," Jesus said. "It's time to sit down. Where do you sit?" Then He laid out the options. If you choose a seat of honor and then someone more distinguished shows up, your host will ask you to move, which will be humiliating. But if you choose a humble seat, your host might insist that you move to a better spot, which would be an honor. Jesus concluded by saying, "For everyone who exalts himself will be humbled, and he who humbles himself will be exalted" (Luke 14:11).

If Jesus was trying to tell these comparison-prone leaders to "just stop," He might have told them a story about going to the wedding blindfolded or finding a seat randomly. But how practical is that? None of us can live life blindfolded to the differences that exist between others and ourselves. Yet we *can* choose the humble seat. And when we do, we free ourselves from the comparison trap.

CHOOSING THE HUMBLE SEAT

Notice that Luke 14:11 says the person who humbles *himself* will be exalted. We often think of "being humbled." We talk about humbling as something that happens *to* us. But in his book, *The End of Me,* Kyle Idleman points out, "Jesus speaks of a humbling that is *active*—we are the humblers. This is not something we wait for to occur naturally. 'Humble yourself.'"

If we want to free ourselves from the comparison trap and stop seeing our teammates as threats, Jesus gives one escape hatch: we must actively pursue humility. It won't happen on its own; we have to choose a humble seat. We have to put others in the seats of honor.

Choosing the humble seat—especially when the stakes are high—has a dramatic effect on our hearts. It frees us from the bondage of superiority and pride, but also from the bondage of jealous insecurity. As an added benefit, when we choose the humble seat, we choose community rather than isolation. We begin seeing others as co-workers, not competition.

I got to enjoy all of these benefits a few years ago, when I made a conscious decision to choose the humble seat. I had just gone through the difficult experience of having a book contract cancelled. My book was to be part of the "Amazing" line of Bible studies published by "Big Christian Publications" (not their real names). But Big Christian was making some department-wide cuts which involved dissolving the Amazing line, and therefore my book. I was heartbroken.

My friend "Melissa" was a huge support and encouragement to me during this time. Melissa had far more experience than I with speaking and writing, and she urged me to keep trusting God. In an email, she shared 1 Peter 4:12-13 from *The Message* paraphrase:

> "Friends, when life gets really difficult, don't jump to the conclusion that God isn't on the job. Instead, be glad that you are in the very thick of what Christ experienced. This is a spiritual refining process, with glory just around the corner."

Melissa continued, "I can't wait to see what God is preparing for you just around the corner!"

I clung to her encouragement and the truth she had shared from God's Word. I trusted that God was "on the job" and I gave myself to the refining process. But I had no idea that part of my refinement would involve choosing a humble seat beside Melissa.

A few months after my book was cancelled, Melissa called me. She shared that Big Christian Publications wanted to publish her next book, but she was hesitant because of me. She said, "Shannon, if you want me to turn it down, I will."

This would have been a big sacrifice for Melissa! Do you see how she was putting my concerns ahead of her own? Because of her sweet humility and loyalty toward me, I didn't feel even the slightest bit of jealousy. I was able to give my wholehearted blessing on Melissa's new assignment.

But a few days later I received two back-to-back emails. The first came from my agent, with news that wasn't good. She had been working tirelessly to find a new publisher for my cancelled book, and after several promising conversations, a smaller publisher—one of the last on my list of hopefuls—had decided to pass on my manuscript. A whole new wave of disappointment and frustration washed over me, which made the next email even harder.

It was from Melissa to a group of friends, sharing the fabulous news about her new book contract. This didn't surprise me, of course, but one part did. Melissa's new book was not only going to be published by Big Christian; it was going to be part of the *Amazing* line—which apparently was *not* being dissolved after all.

Boom. There it was. The powerful temptation to compare.

Why was there room for Melissa's book in the Amazing line, and not mine? Why was she being accepted when I had been rejected? Why did God want her book to be published but not my book? I blinked back tears of resentment and frustration as I stared at my computer screen.

In that moment, my heart screamed for me to recoil from Melissa. *Just delete this email. You need to back away from Melissa's friendship. It hurts too much!*

But then, I sensed the Spirit of God urging me to do exactly the opposite. Melissa had proven herself to be my friend. She was wise and kind and considerate. She had encouraged and supported me in a way that few others could have during this time. And she had even asked for my *blessing* before considering this contract!

So I prayed, "Lord, help me to rejoice with Melissa! Help me to resist the temptation to pull away and lick my wounds. Help me to celebrate what You're doing through Melissa instead."

And then, with God's strength, I made my choice. I chose the humble seat. With tears on my cheeks, I typed a heartfelt note to Melissa, rejoicing over this opportunity that God had provided. I promised to cheer her on every step of the way and support her in any way I could. And do you know what happened? When that email left my computer, every trace of jealousy and resentment was ejected from my heart along with it.

By humbling myself and lifting up my friend, I had unlatched the comparison trap and set myself free.

BUILDING ON

Take a mental snapshot of yourself as an influencer on your platform. There's no need to shrink yourself down or deflate your gifts. That's not humility any more than inflating your importance is. Take an honest look at who you are and what you've been given.

Now zoom out and notice that your platform is resting on top of the massive and unmovable rock of your salvation—Jesus Christ. As a platform builder, you're only adding on to what Christ has already done—which is what other Christian influencers are doing as well.

Zoom out a little wider and notice how your platform connects to the platforms of others. Perhaps you serve alongside blog teammates or ministry co-leaders. Maybe you're part of a group of authors or speakers or ministry workers who live in the same area. Perhaps some of your teammates have large, elevated platforms. Others may have platforms that are barely an inch off the ground. Zoom out even further and include Christian influencers you've never even met.

Do you have your panoramic snapshot? This is your team. These are your brothers and sisters. They are serving your same Jesus in the same ways you do.

As an influencer, if your goal is to measure up, get ahead, or elevate your platform above someone else's, then my friend, you've lost your way. On the other hand, if you feel undone by the successes of others or insignificant and ineffective because your platform is less than impressive, then my friend, you've lost perspective.

But there is something you can do which will pull you back to focus and guard against mission creep: You can humble yourself. You can choose the humble seat. You can free yourself from the comparison trap that only produces superiority, inferiority, and division.

OUR HUMBLE LORD

Jesus is the ultimate example of choosing the humble seat. Philippians 2:7 says that by becoming human, Jesus emptied Himself of status. Jesus counted the very people He created as significant and worth spending Himself on. So much so, He died on the cross that they might have eternal life. And God responded to Christ's humility by lifting Jesus out of that grave, exalting Him, and giving Him the name above every name (Philippians 2:3-11).

And as one who has benefited from Jesus' humility, Philippians 2:3 offers an appropriate response: "Do nothing from selfish ambition or conceit, but in humility count others more significant than yourselves."

Choosing the humble seat involves counting others as more significant. Every time you choose this response, you free yourself from the trap of jealousy, insecurity, and shame. You also free yourself from the trap of pride, conceit, and self-centeredness—and you promote community rather than isolation.

Comparison is a natural part of life, but it doesn't have to be a trap. We can choose to free ourselves by practicing humility.

{CHAPTER EIGHT}

SIFT

"Search me, O God, and know my heart!
Try me and know my thoughts!
And see if there be any grievous way in me,
and lead me in the way everlasting!"
— *Psalm 139:23-24*

"I'm so humbled by...."

I (Shannon) always cringe when I hear a Christian influencer start this way, because they're often about to communicate anything *but* humility. I can say this on some authority because I've used the phrase myself.

"I'm so humbled by the number of readers this piece has attracted."

"I'm so humbled to have such amazing endorsers."

"I'm so humbled by the number of people who came out tonight."

What I mean is, "I really want you to notice how many people like me or approve of me or have validated me, but I don't want you to think I'm an arrogant bragger so I'm making this a humble brag." Somehow it has become acceptable to claim humility at the precise moment we're about to do something a humble person wouldn't: self-promote.

Self-promotion, especially among influencers, is not only accepted; it's expected. Any fledgling writer, speaker, or leader is expected to be tweeting about every success, posting about every event, and Instagramming photos with well-known people. If we—their would-be audience— Google their name and come up dry, we wonder who in the world they think they're going to influence, because the world is using social media.

This all makes sense from a pragmatic, marketing perspective. But as Christians, Kate and I struggle with the idea of self-promotion. We're guessing you do, too.

BLIND INFLUENCERS

Christ says that to follow Him, we must deny ourselves, not *promote* ourselves. We must take up our cross, not take up our rankings. We must lay our lives down, not lift ourselves up.

So what does Jesus think of my attempts to attract subscribers with pop-up opt-ins and gather "likes" on my Facebook author page? Is He pleased with my attempts to widen my reach and spread the truth? Actually, we can hear from Jesus directly on this matter, by considering His response to some first century, God-appointed influencers— the keepers of the scrolls.

The scribes and Pharisees were entrusted with the role of keeping God's pure Word from error. People didn't have scrolls for themselves. The Pharisees read and interpreted the Scriptures for them. And how did this role impact the Pharisees' hearts? What was the result?

Unfortunately, they fell headlong into the trap of self-promotion by using their influence to lift up themselves, not God. Jesus said that they were blind men leading other blind men straight into a pit. And what were the scribes and Pharisees blind to? *Themselves.* They didn't see just how offensive they had become toward God.

Here's what Jesus said to them:

> "Woe to you, scribes and Pharisees, hypocrites! For you clean the outside of the cup and the plate, but inside they are full of greed and self-indulgence. You blind Pharisee! First clean the inside of the cup and the plate, that the outside also may be clean." (Matthew 23:25-26)

Our greatest danger is to project light out to others, but remain blind to ourselves. When we become blind, puffed up influencers, we lead others—not to Jesus—but into a pit. We need the Holy Spirit to shine a spotlight onto each tiny speck of pride, which threatens to spread like mold and contaminate even our best intentions.

Thankfully, the Holy Spirit is more than happy to show us the "inside of the cup." He shines His mega-voltage conviction deeply into our hearts, revealing pride, greed, and self-indulgence. And He often uses tangible surface evidence to reveal our undetected sin. Our words, in particular—whether written or spoken—reveal our hearts (Luke 6:45). In this way, social media works to our advantage.

A LOOK INSIDE THE CUP

Social media provides a unique mirror to our hearts. Every opportunity to post is a new opportunity for the Spirit to show us the "inside of the cup." Every tool to measure our audience's response offers a tool to measure our motives. Every chance to gain a follower is another chance to become a more intentional follower of Jesus. These opportunities to peer into our "inner cup" with the help of the

Spirit are gifts. We don't want to allow our pride to grow the way the Pharisees' did. We don't want to become blind to our own arrogance and selfishness. With every nail we pound into our expanding platforms, we want to see our hearts clearly.

We need *Jesus* to provide the specs for our platform-building efforts. Before we influence others, let's be influenced by Him! As we get to work on our platforms, let's learn to swing a hammer the way Jesus did—with humility and service, not pride and greed. Let's change the world, but not in the way the world says. Let's gather followers the way Jesus would, by laying our lives down, rather than lifting ourselves up.

SLIPPERY SLOPE

One night I opened an email from a woman I had never met, who was thanking me for a post I had written for the True Woman blog, yet her message didn't mention True Woman. Instead, she referenced a certain ministry page on Facebook—one that I had never heard of.

Pleasantly surprised that a ministry had shared my writing, I opened my phone and searched for the ministry's Facebook page. There it was! My post, with about a dozen "likes" and comments below it. I was delighted.

I immediately wondered if others, too, had shared this post. I decided to search for the article's title on Facebook and my eyes widened in surprise at the resulting list of individuals and organizations who had shared my writing. As I read their glowing comments and responses to my work, a grin began to spread across my face.

My grin got wider with every click, tap, and swipe. I silently wondered how many people had read what I had written. Hundreds? Thousands? My heart swelled with pride! Then suddenly I remembered something—I remembered what the article was about.

SERVING YOU OR SERVING ME?

I had written about hardship and struggle, and I had done so after God opened my eyes to a particular truth from Scripture. I remembered back to that day, when I had typed out the message that resonated so deeply within me. Tears streamed as I had pictured the readers who might find comfort, clarity, and hope in the message God had given me to share. With their burdens and pain in mind, I had spun my words together, thinking, *Oh Lord! How I long for others to see and delight in this truth!*

But in the weeks between writing the article and receiving the email about it, the tears in my eyes had dried up. Now, instead of crying, I was grinning. Rather than imagining the burdens carried by readers on the opposite side of my screen, I was imagining how *many* people had gathered there. I had gone from Christ-like serving to devilish self-exaltation. The discovery made me sick.

Have you ever detected a similar progression in yourself? Author and pastor Kevin DeYoung puts it this way:

> "Do I want money and recognition? Do I feel the need for validation? Do I like it when I look successful? Or do I want people to learn more about Christ and honor him with their lives? Yes, yes, yes, and yes. I pray that my heart is mostly concerned with the last yes, but sometimes it's hard to tell."[14]

I can completely relate. Can you? When you invest in writing, speaking, serving, or leading, do you ever experience a shift in motives?

Maybe you set out to start a blog for fellow moms of adopted kids, but then found yourself obsessing over comments from readers gushing about your wisdom and advice. Or maybe you started an organization to feed orphans, but you found yourself enjoying the elevated opinions of others who admire how you've served. Perhaps you opened your home to lead a Bible study, but then heard yourself almost bragging about the way the group quickly out-grew the space in your living room. What began as a pure desire to serve others, share your gifts, or give sacrificially started to morph—without you realizing it—into a desire to serve yourself, receive recognition, or get validation.

SHIFTING MOTIVES

We aren't the first to experience a shift in motives. Consider these examples of Bible characters who set out to serve the Lord, then fell prey to the undertow of self-focus:

- David, who loved God and longed to serve Him, wrongly took a census—counting what belonged to God, not himself. (1 Chronicles 21)

- Aaron, who was given the honor of serving as Israel's priest, crafted a golden calf to please the impatient people. (Exodus 32)

- The disciples, who had left everything to follow Jesus, had regular arguments about who was the greatest. (Luke 9:46)

Clearly, this fickle waffling between serving the Lord and serving self is not a new phenomenon. Back in 1948, A.W. Tozer wrote, "Promoting self under the guise of promoting Christ is currently so common as to excite little notice." As Solomon taught, there is nothing new under the sun (Ecclesiastes 1:9). However, these old problems are surely amplified by the unique challenges presented in social media.

Like the printing press of King James' day, the internet and social media are tools used to mass produce great quantities of material, both good and bad. We, as Christian influencers, can use these tools for good! If we didn't capitalize on these opportunities, we would be like the man in Jesus' parable, who buried his talent rather than investing it (Matthew 25:14-30).

However, while social media has opened new windows and gates for sharing what's good, there's something about all of those open windows and gates that creates a draft for my heart. How easily I am swept along toward the sin of self-focus.

No longer am I simply the sower, reaching into my sack of seed for bits of truth and encouragement to scatter out to a hungry world. I become the sower who tosses something out, then receives something *back*—often in two seconds flat. Perhaps someone retweets what I've said. My photos get "likes" or comments. My writing gets shared. With every click, swipe, and share, I receive tangible evidence that people not only like my message; that they like *me*.

So while social media can be like a mirror in the Spirit's hand to show me my heart, it can also be like a fog machine filling the murky rooms of my heart. *Why* do I share the post I've written? *Why* do I tweet out truth about Jesus? *Why* do I share Instagram photos of giant stacks of my books? Do I do so because I want to serve Jesus? Or is my desire to serve myself?

THE VALUE OF THE SEARCH

It's okay to feel conflicted. It's okay to wrestle in prayer over platform-building decisions, seeking discernment and wisdom from above. Trevin Wax of The Gospel Coalition articulates the benefit of this struggle:

> "I'm still conflicted about blogging about my book. Maybe that's where I need to be. Maybe this is the Spirit's method of rooting out sinful motivations and spurring me on to holiness. Maybe God is saying, 'I don't ever want you to be totally comfort-

able with self-promotion, even if some promotion will result in more people buying a book that is beneficial to the church.' Maybe God wants me to remember that my motives are never completely pure, and even my best intentions are tainted with sin."[15]

Wrestling with the issue of platform-building is a profitable exercise. There is value in working through these questions and weighing our motives. Kate and I have even come to the place where we thank God for the blessed tension that He has placed in our hearts.

UNITE MY HEART

In Psalm 86:11, David asked God to unite his heart so he might fear the Lord and walk in truth. If David asked God for a "united heart," it was because he realized that his heart was divided. Part of him wanted one thing, and another part wanted something else. He had conflicting motivations, just like so many of us regularly do.

Often this is the case when we seek to serve the Lord, but especially when we take steps to expand our ministries in new ways. Our pure motives and tainted ones get all jumbled up together.

As you either consider the efforts you're already making to build your platform and share your work, or as you contemplate new ways of stepping out to spread the light of Jesus, let me encourage you to first turn the light inward. Take some time to examine your efforts—especially your attempts to leverage social media to spread truth. Ask God, like David did, to unite your heart so that you might fear the Lord and walk in truth.

As you reflect, I invite you to use a tool I've designed to help evaluate my own heart, which I call the "Heart Sifter."

THE HEART SIFTER

As I write, one of my friends is waiting to hear back from the agent she would like to represent her. Another friend is putting together a "speaker page" on her website. Still another is waiting to hear back from a publisher on his first novel.

What brave new steps are you considering, today? What platform-building decisions are you trying to make? Each choice you make will be driven by motives—often conflicting ones. The Heart Sifter is designed to help you sort out the good motives from the bad so you have clarity on how to proceed.

Consider setting aside an hour or two to work through this activity. Give yourself the time you need to really take a look at your heart.

Here's how it works:

Create a diagram like this one (or print one out at www.shannonpopkin.com/influence):

Option A	Option B:
+	+
–	–

List the two options you're trying to decide between at the top. Often these two options will simply be taking this new step versus not taking it.

In the "plus" box underneath each option, list out the

positives for making that particular choice. These are "reasons for" choosing this option. Do the same with the negatives for each column in the corresponding "minus" box. These are "reasons against" that choice.

Here's an example of what your chart might look like as you begin:

Option A Work with an Agent	Option B: Work on My Own
+ Credibility with other authors. Don't have to promote myself. Agents have connections. Publishers appreciate agents vetting authors.	**+** No negative emotions if I'm rejected. Full autonomy. Reliance on God.
— I have to rely on the agent. What if he doesn't push for my success?	**—** I don't know any publishers. What if my proposal is lacking?

Empty out each of your heart motives onto the paper. Be honest and thorough. Take your time. Ask God to help you sift your heart and consider each of your motivations separately.

Now, here's the most important part: Go back and evaluate each motivation behind the reasons you have listed in the four quadrants. Write your motivation beside each one.

Here's what your diagram might look like:

Option A Work with an Agent	Option B: Work on My Own
+ Credibility with other authors. → *Insecurity* Don't have to promote myself. → *False humility* Agents have connections. → *Craving control* Publishers appreciate agents vetting authors. → *Consideration and humility*	**+** No negative emotions if I'm rejected. → *Inadequacy* Full autonomy. → *Control* Reliance on God. → *Trust*
— I have to rely on the agent. → *Fear* What if he doesn't push for my success? → *Selfishness*	**—** I don't know any publishers. → *Insecurity* What if my proposal is lacking? → *Insecurity*

Once you have all of the heart motivations listed beside each positive and negative, get out a thick black marker. Cross out any motivation that is driven by something that God wouldn't use to motivate you. Look for things like:

- Fear

- Insecurity

- Selfishness

- False humility

- Inadequacy

As you do this, surrender these false motivators, which are not from God.

Now, look at what is left standing. These are the right

motivations of your heart! Your decision should be made based on these motivators, not the ones behind the black ink.

When you eliminate wrong motives from your decision making, you can see how God is leading you. You aren't held back by fear or doubt. You aren't driven by selfishness or approval addiction. You're free to do whatever God wants!

One word of caution: Crossing off a false motivator with a black marker does not mean you're finished with it. (I wish!) Even the most godly person must continue to check for creeping selfishness, fear, pride, and doubt. But the Heart Sifter is a multiple-use tool.

As we eliminate false motivators, we unite our hearts to serve and elevate the Lord—not ourselves—in bold, new, creative ways.

IT'S TIME TO PICK A SIDE

Obviously, it's nice to see our group of followers grow. It's nice to see our books sell and our events packed and ministries thrive under our leadership. But the affirmation we receive from other people can be very addictive. The praise of other people is a strong undertow that can pull us away from our original mission to elevate Jesus.

That day my blog post was appearing all over social media, I couldn't maintain both my selfish grin and my compassionate tears at the same time. I had to make a choice. Was I going to celebrate Jesus' glory or my own?

Author Tony Reinke offers this heart check challenge: "If the glory of man is your god, you will not celebrate the glory of Christ. Or, if you come to Christ and treasure his glory above all other glory, you will be forced to forfeit the buzz of human approval."[16]

This is true when things are going my way, but it's *especially* true when they aren't. As you know, some of the truths Jesus might prompt me to share have the potential of creating the wrong kind of buzz on social media. What then? Will I follow Jesus even if it means I lose followers?

Reinke points out the harsh reality: "If you want to follow Christ, the world will unfollow you."[17] That's just the way it is—and truthfully, the way it should be. But we must fear the disapproval of God far more than we fear the disappearance of our online followers.[18] Reinke continues, "You will be shunned. You will be despised." John Piper puts it even more bluntly, stating that we cannot serve two masters. We cannot serve both the praise of man and the praise of God (ibid).

As Christians, we've got to pick a side. We've got to decide. Are we committed to elevating Christ or elevating ourselves?

{CHAPTER NINE}

SERVE

"If you want to lift yourself up, lift up someone else."
— Booker T. Washington

After spending years chasing and implementing ways to establish a noteworthy online platform for myself, I (Kate) found some advice from a fellow Christian that changed my entire outlook. It sounds simple, but I really hadn't thought about it this way before.

Author, speaker, and professor Karen Swallow Prior offers this pointed challenge: "Ignore what social media experts tell you about using social media to build 'platform.' Instead, use social media to serve people."

What a liberating perspective and strategy! Rather than viewing platform building as an obligation to succeed, I can view it as an opportunity to serve. Instead of sharing content with the intention of building my own platform, I can choose to build others up.

When I make this shift in my focus and intentions, my

entire attitude about social media and platform building changes for the better. Now, instead of seeing it as a rigid requirement necessary for growth and success, I can see it as a strategic way to be a blessing to others, to meet new friends, to help and encourage people, to spread hope, and ultimately to glorify God with the gifts I've been given.

I love the perspective of these three writers:

> "I felt seriously gross about platform building until I changed how I look at it. Now I see it as relationship building. Because of that perspective shift, I've made some amazing friends online and am able to encourage them. It's all about how you see what you're doing."
>
> *— Susie Finkbeiner*

> "Platform building only gets gross when we make it the focus of attention. When we shift our focus to metrics, we've lost. Instead, as writers and speakers, our focus is always on serving and relating. We show up and say, 'I made this. Here, it's for you.'"
>
> *— Emily P. Freeman*

> "Most days I just want to quit. The thing that keeps me going is the burning desire to help people through my words. It isn't about my worth, it's about the reader's worth. They are worth my best efforts."
>
> *— Christy Rood*

I've discovered that it's not about how high I can climb on the ladder of man-made success. It's about how I can offer myself as a means for others to climb the ladder toward eternity with Christ. Maybe that means leaning down into the waters of despair, stretching myself on the dock with arms fully extended so tired swimmers can grasp the rungs to reach dry land. Or maybe it means standing firm in the sand where my feet are planted, holding tight to the lifeguard ladder while someone else ascends the steps to assume their God-given position above me.

Author and speaker Ann Voskamp said it well: "We aren't here to one-up one another, but to help one another up. Aspiring to success isn't about reaching up ladders—it's about reaching out and aspiring to serve."[19]

Best of all, by taking this posture of service, we grow closer toward imitating our Master. For "whoever would be great among you must be your servant, and whoever would be first among you must be slave of all. For even the Son of Man came not to be served but to serve, and to give his life as a ransom for many" (Mark 10:43b-45).

UNEXPECTED BENEFITS

On October 21, 2017, I watched a Hurricane Relief Benefit Concert that took place at Texas A&M University. All five living former U.S. presidents attended the concert to show support and raise funds for those affected by recent hurricanes. At one point during the event, the emcee called five civilians onto the stage to be recognized for their selfless and significant relief efforts after the storms. As I watched each person make their way down the line of presidents, stopping to shake each man's hand, I thought, *Wow. That's quite an honor to meet all five living former presidents at one time!*

When those people helped with the aftermath of the hurricanes, they had no idea that they would one day receive such an opportunity. They weren't acting like Pharisees, doing good deeds for the sake of being seen and praised. Like the Mystery Sandcastle Masters, they just did the work. That's what true service looks like.

While I've never received such substantial recognition, I have experienced countless unexpected benefits from serving. Soon after I started thinking about the best interests of my audience above my own, I was pleasantly surprised by the way others were drawn toward the change. By lifting others instead of myself, I discovered I was actually attracting a larger community of sincere, engaged followers. It sounds counterintuitive, especially by the world's standards, but it really is possible to see growth in your platform while using it as a space and means to elevate others. When I started intentionally sharing content that I thought would be helpful to my followers, more people started liking, sharing, and commenting on the posts, which in turn resulted in higher visibility because of increased engagement. See the pleasant ripple effect that can occur when we take the focus off ourselves?

Think about it: As a reader, consumer, and social media user, aren't you naturally drawn to those people who splash kindness and generosity across your screen? As one indwelled by the Holy Spirit, ask Him to help you display His fruit in your interactions online. You can't go wrong by consistently practicing love, joy, peace, patience, kindness, goodness, faithfulness, gentleness, and self-control (Galatians 5:22-23) as you post on your website and on social media. It's kind of like that principle from Matthew 6:33, "Seek first the kingdom of God and his righteousness, and all these things will be added unto you."

I've also been pleasantly surprised by the genuine relationships I've built from online connections. Some of the most spiritually encouraging conversations I have each week are with people I met on the internet. Also, I happen to love supporting other speakers and writers online as much as I can. I love promoting other people's books, products, quotes, and blog posts. As a result, when the time came for my own book to release, I had such an incredible support system of people ready and willing to help. Of course that wasn't the *reason* I've helped spread the word about other people's work, but it was definitely an added encouragement along the way.

THE PURSUIT OF EXCELLENCE

We've touched quite a bit on using online channels to promote the gospel and elevate the name of Christ, but what if you're a Christian writer or speaker who doesn't necessarily write or speak for the Christian market? Is it still possible to serve God and your audience if you're not sharing "spiritual" material? In my opinion, absolutely. If you're a believer in Christ, it's essential that you maintain your Christian witness and testimony no matter what you say or write—and I believe one way of doing that is by pursuing excellence in all that you do. You can bring glory to God simply by giving your best effort—even if that doesn't end up in a book deal or public speaking engagement.

Author and speaker Dan Darling encourages, "Let's attempt to discern between a platform building that is sinful and a godly ambition that is good. There is a kind of platform building and an encouragement of platform building that is sinful and antithetical to the gospel. A kind of soul-less self-promotion and a desire to be 'something' and find validation in the affirmation of the crowds. This is a temptation that affects all of us in this digital age.... We need to fight this every day by dying to ourselves and living for Jesus.... We should fight the desire to be something. We should remember that we will one day die, the work of the kingdom will go on, and most people will not remember our names.

However, there is an ambition that is not sinful. We should not confuse the above fame-seeking with a genuine desire to serve the body of Christ with our gifts. A willingness to serve—via our writing or speaking or preaching—is a good thing (1 Timothy 3:1). We should strive, in whatever vocation we are called, to do things with excellence to glorify God (Colossians 3:23)."[20]

GIVE YOUR GIFT

Remember that phenomenal sandcastle I told you about in the chapter on pride? Well, that night after we left the beach, a thunderstorm rolled in. Lightning flashed, thunder cracked and boomed, and rain pelted down in sheets.

The next day, my husband left the house early in the morning to go for a walk to the beach. To his surprise, the Mystery Sandcastle Masters were at it again—this time, with a brand new creation. The storm had destroyed their original masterpiece, but they remained undeterred. The tireless sculptors were there to make art.

A few days later, our whole family returned to the beach one more time before the school year began and summer faded away. To our delight, yet *another* sandcastle was waiting for us to admire. As we stood next to it, taking in every detail, a woman walked up and asked us, "Did you make this?"

We said no, and proceeded to tell her about the previous works of art we had witnessed in recent days. "That's amazing," the woman gushed. "They just leave their creations here for everyone walking by to enjoy. It's like a gift."

As those crafted in the image of God, you and I also have gifts to offer. Maybe you're not skilled with a chisel or carving knife to craft ornate structures from packed sand, but through your writing, speaking, teaching, and leading gifts, you have the ability to create art. You might never know who walks by to enjoy it—and that's okay. That's not always for us to know. As Emily P. Freeman said earlier in this chapter, you have the opportunity to show up and say, "I made this. Here, it's for you."

Gifts are meant to be given. What's keeping you from offering yours?

BE THE LIGHT

We all know that the internet and social media in particular can be a dark, depressing place. Sometimes it's downright nasty. The screen provides a sense of anonymity and sometimes bravery (if we can call it that) which often make people say things they wouldn't have the guts to say in person—and as a result, people can get mean online. Really mean. Storms can roll in overnight, people can boom out thunderous remarks and threats, and the pelting rain of negativity can threaten to wash away even your best efforts.

The positive side is that through technology we now have the ability to reach thousands—even millions—with the click of a button. We no longer need to wait for a literary agent or traditional publisher to offer us a dotted line on which to sign—the internet itself is a form of instant publishing. This is an incredible opportunity—and a weighty responsibility. How will you use it? More importantly, how can you use it to *serve*?

WAITING TABLES

My kids love setting up a lemonade stand during the summer or whenever we have a garage sale. They spend an entire morning baking yummy treats and mixing up cold lemonade and iced tea to serve to passersby, then haul everything outside to display on a folding table on the side of the road. They typically do really well, especially when the sun is shining and temperatures are high. But on one particular garage sale day, the weather was not in their favor. In spite of the cool breeze and dark clouds, my kids got all set up outside. People who stopped to see what we had for sale were pulling their jackets close to block the cold wind. They glanced at the lemonade stand and kept walking. Disappointed, my kids realized, "We should have made hot chocolate instead of lemonade!"

Serving your reader or listener might look a bit like having a lemonade stand or working as a waiter or waitress in a restaurant. It's going to be hard work, and it might not always go as well as you hope. Also, it's important to remember that no restaurant or lemonade stand has an unlimited number of items available; each one has a set menu from which customers can choose. Take some time to determine what it is you have to offer, and what your audience is most likely to want.

What's on your menu of items you'd like to dish out to your readers and listeners? What are you good at preparing and serving? Which dish is your specialty? What does the weather look like on the other side of your screen or microphone? In other words, what's going to be most appealing to your audience right now? Do they need a plate full of hope during a dark season? Do they need a cold glass of humor in the midst of frustration? Or do they need a sweet treat to help them swallow a bitter providence?

My kids didn't make sushi or escargot to sell at their lemonade stand, because that's not (yet) in their wheelhouse. They stuck with what they knew they were good at. Similarly, they didn't attempt to sell school photos of themselves—they labored over chocolate-covered Rice Krispies treats and brownies with cookie dough to entice potential customers. And it worked!

Once you've established your menu, tie an apron around your waist and be the best server you can be—cheerful, efficient, patient, and attentive, delivering the best spiritual food you have to offer. Make it your goal to have your followers leave your establishment feeling full, nourished, and eager to come back again—rain or shine.

HEART CHECK

As you consider posting content to your website or social media account, here are some questions to ask yourself first:

1. Am I posting this to serve myself or to serve other people?

2. Does this post bring glory to God, or tarnish the name of Christ?

3. Am I sharing this to build my platform or to build community?

4. If the idea of platform building still feels yucky to me, what can I do to shift my perspective toward a more positive mindset?

5. How can I use the opportunities I've been given through the internet and social media as a means of serving others and Christ?

PRACTICAL TIPS

You might still be wondering, "Okay, but what do I *do*? How do I practically serve other people online? What am I supposed to post on social media that will lift other people up?"

One easy option as you get started is to find other social media profiles with beautifully decorated quotes, then sharing those to your own page with the appropriate credit. This is a simple way to sprinkle light and hope within your sphere of influence.

You could also make a practice of sharing blog posts, articles, or book reviews written by other people, as opposed to only publishing your own content. Invite people to guest post on your website if you have one. Leave reviews on Amazon for books you've enjoyed. Ask questions and set up polls on social media to gauge your readers' interests and needs, then create content to answer those questions or help solve their problems. Start a weekly prayer thread—ask the simple question, "How can I be praying for you today?" then take time to lift those requests before the Lord.

Highlight the accomplishments and achievements of other brothers and sisters in Christ when you notice jobs well done. Leave encouraging comments on blog posts or articles that you read. Share quotes from your favorite books or articles on Twitter, Instagram, or Facebook. Post a daily or weekly Bible verse to inject truth into the web. The list is endless. The main emphasis is to take the focus off yourself and turn it toward God and His people.

Lastly, a parting challenge: Grab a pen and paper and jot down this motto to display near your workspace: Seek to serve.

CHAPTER TEN

NETWORK

"Let another praise you, and not your own mouth;
a stranger, and not your own lips."
— Proverbs 27:2

Just this year, I (Shannon) have had the joy of seeing my first book published. As part of that process, I was required to ask for endorsements for the book. This was not comfy or fun for me. I've always been reluctant to ask for ministry recommendations, or to introduce my work to other leaders. I don't want to seem pushy or assertive. And I especially don't want to seem as if I'm self-promoting!

But guess what I've been learning about endorsements? The Bible is full of them!

ENDORSEMENTS: THEN AND NOW

The Church was born after Jesus rose from the dead. The Church movement began as people fanned out from Jerusalem in response to persecution.

Back then, there were Jewish Pharisees claiming that Jesus was not God. Then there were the Jewish Jesus followers saying that Jesus *was* God—and that He was the only way to be reconciled to the Lord. And then, there were non-Jewish people who had heard the gospel in their own languages and were sharing it with joy to their own people!

All of this created a huge margin for error. False teachers popped up everywhere. The church leaders needed to vet people and guard the truth. As God-appointed shepherds, they were tasked with tending the flock of prone-to-wander new believers.

So what method did they come up with for guarding the churches in their care? Endorsements. The New Testament is peppered with them! Repeatedly, we hear of leaders in the church networking with each other and recommending one another for ministry.

Here are just a few of many examples:

- Paul tried to contact disciples in Jerusalem, but they feared him because of his murderous past. So Barnabas walked Paul in, validated his conversion story, and recommended him for ministry. (Acts 9:26-30)

- Paul told the Colossians to welcome John Mark (Colossians 4:10), which indicates a restored relationship after the conflict in Acts 15:36-37. Obviously John Mark had earned back Paul's trust.

- Paul chose Timothy as a partner in ministry based on the recommendations of the brothers at Lystra and Iconium. (Acts 16:2)

There are also plenty of examples of leaders in the church warning *against* false teachers or those with selfish motives. Giving and relying on endorsements is one way for leaders to be protective of God's people.

FIVE GUIDELINES

As an influencer in the Church (and that is what we all are), asking to be recommended or endorsed can feel pushy or self-promoting. But it's important to remember that just as with the early believers, endorsements are a biblical way for leaders to safeguard the Church.

I didn't have a choice about asking for book endorsements, which actually made it more comfortable for me. I could say, "My publisher has asked…." But what about when we *do* have a choice? Should we be proactive about asking for new opportunities to speak, write, or lead? Should we reach out to people who have more influence than we do? Or should we wait on God to open doors? I would argue that we should do both.

Here are some guidelines that I've found helpful:

1. **Focus on the opportunities that God *has* given.**

   Rather than putting so much emphasis on the ways you *hope* God will use you, commit yourself to the assignments you already have. Be responsible. Serve well. Be passionate. Pour yourself into the opportunities God *has* granted—whether that be teaching the Bible story to preschoolers, speaking at a small retreat, or ministering to your own family.

   Karen Swallow Prior, a professor at Liberty University, says, "I've never met an aspiring pro athlete who isn't putting in thousands of hours learning, improving, and perfecting her skills. But I've met more than a few aspiring writers more concerned with seeking a platform than with practicing their craft or discerning a needed message."

Whatever our calling, we need to be faithful in crafting our work, and put God in charge of the timetable for expanding our ministries.

About a decade ago, I was asked to be one of the rotating teachers for my women's Bible study group. I was delighted, and poured every last drop of my extra time and passion into serving the forty-some women in our group. I dug deep into Scripture, researched, listened to sermons, and read commentaries. I spent hours writing and rewriting my lessons. I would distill my message, weed out side notes, smooth transitions, craft illustrations, and funnel everything into one main point of application. I wanted to pack as much truth as I possibly could into my allotted twenty minutes, for the sake of my sisters who would graciously give me their attention.

Looking back, I can see that my preparation work *then* was preparing me for my writing assignments now. As I work on my current assignment—writing Bible studies—I still labor over the distillment of each message, transitions, and funneling each lesson toward an application, but the process has become a lot more intuitive. And when I divide up my Bible study material into individual lessons, guess how much content I pack into each one? The equivalent of about one of my twenty-minute teaching sessions for my former Bible study group.

I'm convinced that if I hadn't put so much energy into *that* assignment, I wouldn't be nearly as ready for this one.

2. Listen to input.

Because of our pride, insecurities, and selfishness, it's often incredibly difficult to see ourselves accurately. We need others in the body of Christ to hold up a mirror and tell us what they see in us. Sometimes this means being encouraged to try a role we feel inadequate for. Other times it means being redirected away from a role that we aren't gifted for. Relying on input from other believers is one way of letting God point us toward the good works that He has prepared in advance for each of us to do (Ephesians 2:10).

About a year ago, I did a webinar for the first time, and one of the women who attended was Leslie Bennett, the managing editor for the Revive Our Hearts' Leader Connection. Leslie has far more ministry experience than I do, so afterward I asked for her input on the webinar. In years past, I might have been hesitant to do so. I had been clumsy with the technology. I had a terrible cold that day. It really wasn't my best work, but I decided to humble myself and receive whatever feedback Leslie offered. I was so glad I did. What a gold mine of advice!

Here's what Leslie suggested:

- Setting an end time so participants would know the time commitment. (How had I missed this important detail?)

- Condensing my illustrations. (Yes! I wasn't speaking to an audience; I was leading a discussion. You tell stories differently in conversation than from a platform.)

- Having some pre-written questions in case participants didn't submit any. (Brilliant! Sometimes providing one question gets the ball rolling.)

- Closing in prayer. (Oh, how I wished I had thought to do this!)

Leslie was so helpful. I have referred back to her input several times. Plus, she blessed me with lots of encouragement, and that conversation has led to other opportunities to write for the blog Leslie manages.

Having the eyes of other Christ-following influencers on our work is invaluable. Don't miss out on the growth opportunities that will be yours when you welcome and listen to input.

3. Be patient.

A couple of years ago, after being told that having a "national" speaking ministry was the next step for me, I made it my goal to stretch my reach over state lines. Here was my strategy. I made a list of cities which had direct flights of $200 or less, and scoured the internet looking for churches in those cities. I searched through websites, seeking to understand each individual ministry and reached out to dozens of church leaders with information about me and my speaking ministry. And guess what happened?

Nothing.

I spent about a month working on all of this, with absolutely no fruit. But you know what *did* happen? Slowly and gradually, I began receiving speaking requests across state lines. Ohio, Wisconsin, Indiana, Illinois. Just last week, I was invited to speak in California. From Michigan, that's *way* over state lines, and I'm guessing the flight will cost more than $200.

None of these speaking requests have resulted from anything but faithfully pouring myself into the *local* opportunities I've been given to speak, and patiently waiting on the Lord to open doors in churches farther away.

Am I saying it's wrong for you to network with friends or to "cold call" or solicit invitations to speak or write or serve? No, but I *am* saying that your efforts might not produce the fruit you desire. Rather than rushing ahead like I did, seek the Lord. Ask Him to direct your networking plans and to produce the lasting fruit that only He can—both in your audience and in you. And remember that waiting before the Lord with a patient heart will *always* produce lasting, spiritual fruit (Galatians 5:22-23).

Looking back, I can see that it was by God's design that my speaking ministry didn't launch like a rocket. Instead it has grown like a fruit tree, year by year, right along with the pace of my skill and family life. Five years ago, my three kids were in elementary, middle, and high school. I would have panicked at the thought of speaking four times in one weekend, given all I had to juggle. With the busy pace of our family, it worked best for me to speak during the day at moms' groups or at the occasional local evening event—which is exactly what I did.

But now that my youngest child is in high school, flying to California for a few days seems more feasible. I've gained enough experience that while speaking for a weekend retreat is taxing, it isn't overwhelming. It's my joy!

If I could speak softly to myself back when I was checking flights and scouring church websites, here's what I would say: *Don't worry about the timeline. Just be patient and trust the Lord to open the doors that He wants you to walk through in His timing, not your own.*

4. Pursue mentoring.

I first met Pearl after I spoke at her church. She shared how much my message had meant to her, then a few months later she contacted me. She had recently started blogging and wondered if I had any advice for her.

I suggested that Pearl attend a local conference where I was scheduled to speak, and she came! Afterward, Pearl followed up with a blog post about her experience at the conference and asked if I would read it over. I gave several suggestions, and she not only followed my advice, she *appreciated* it!

When it was time for my book release, Pearl was one of the first to volunteer for my launch team—and she went above and beyond. She even staged some photos of herself with her nose in my book, and a caption that read, "If anyone needs me, I'll be reading *Control Girl!*" I had a blast sharing such fun photos.

About a year later, when I felt that it was time to hire an assistant, guess who I called? Pearl, of course. She has been an absolute delight to work with. One of the things

I told Pearl when we began working together was, "I'm so sorry I can't pay you what you deserve. But I would love to supplement your income with mentoring!"

Pearl has some quiet dreams about speaking and writing. It has been my delight to offer coaching to help instill confidence. I also love giving Pearl a look at what I do behind the scenes. (I would have been delighted with that opportunity when I was just starting out!)

Pearl is a gem, and I'm privileged to be part of her platform-growing story.

If you're trying to network with someone who is a bit further down the road than you are, consider doing what Pearl did. Make a personal connection. Ask for input. Offer your support and then go above and beyond. Receive mentoring for what it is—a gift offered by someone who cares about you and is willing to offer both their friendship and support.

5. **Trust God.**

When I recounted my "foreword" for you in Chapter Four, I mentioned Chris, the camp director who listened in while I told stories to my campers and encouraged me to write those stories down. Chris became a lifelong mentor and friend to me, and years after I worked for him, he became an author. When I first tried my hand at writing, Chris was kind enough to encourage me and give input on many of my first writing pieces.

I also mentioned Del, who published my first magazine article. What I didn't mention was that Del is married to my college roommate, Debbie. Debbie and Del are the ones who first helped me connect with Revive Our Hearts—the ministry for which I now serve as a contributing blogger.

As I look back, you know what amazes me? I didn't choose my summer job or my roommate based on the way I hoped they might one day help me. At that point, I had no idea that I wanted to be a writer. Yet even then, God was strategically putting my network in place. He was weaving together friendships with people who would one day help me get where God wants me to go. And God is doing the same for you.

You don't have to be pushy or self-promoting. You can trust that your God has a plan for His Church, and you're part of it. Before networking even occurred to you, God's plans were being established (Proverbs 16:9).

PUTTING GOD IN CHARGE

Networking among Christian influencers is a natural part of linking arms in solidarity and protecting the flock against false teaching—but our networking must not be characterized by pushiness or selfishness.

Sometimes at Christian speaking or writing conferences when I watch attendees edging in on each other with their best foot forward, I think we must all look like kids on an Easter egg hunt—aggressively asserting ourselves and trying to gather the most candy. Instead, what if we thought of those conferences as treasure hunts prepared by God for each person there? What if every random conversation—with the person across your table at lunch or beside you in the plenary session or in line behind you outside the bathroom—had the potential of offering a new networking clue? What if you viewed every person you met not as new competition, but new clarity on God's next ministry assignment?

This very thing happened with this book, in fact. Kate and I first got to know each other when a Christian Writers Conference coordinator asked us to work together on a platform-building breakout session. As we prepared our presentation, I kept noticing how God had led Kate and me to similar conclusions. After the conference, I asked Kate, "Would you ever want to write a book together on this topic?" And just like that, I found another clue in this network-enhanced treasure hunt that God has laid out for me.

So don't fret about how to get the attention of a publisher. Don't wring your hands, wondering if you'll ever be asked to speak to a larger audience. Don't badger people to recommend you. Instead, trust in the Lord with all your heart and don't lean on your own understanding of how to advance your ministry or build a larger platform. In all your ways, acknowledge Him as the inspiration and source of power behind your ministry, and He will direct your paths (from Proverbs 3:5-6).

{CHAPTER ELEVEN}

FOCUS

*"…seek first the kingdom of God and his righteousness,
and all these things will be added to you."*
– Matthew 6:33

In this digital age of smartphones and social media, we are constantly bombarded by voices, noise, and distractions. Even if we muster up the self-control to switch off our devices, the demands of everyday life abound. If we're not intentional about our planning, priorities, and time management, it can be very difficult to focus on what is most important in life.

I (Kate) find this particularly true when it comes to online interaction. Even if I tell myself, "I'm just signing on to Facebook to send one message," the next thing I know, twenty minutes have passed and I'm reading reviews about the best lunchboxes for my kids' lunch…without having sent the message I logged on to send.

Particularly when it comes to platform building efforts,

the advice and suggestions are endless—buy this course, run that campaign, pay for this tool, host that giveaway, get more reviews, sign up for these newsletters, set up that ad, send that promotional material, schedule those shares… the list goes on and on. I frequently feel the pressure to be doing more, which only results in a perpetual state of overwhelm and very little productivity. Yet I still give in to the temptation and before I know it, I'm bending over backwards, standing on my head, forking over cash…whatever it takes to gain more followers and earn the attention of that elusive literary agent, publisher, or conference coordinator. *Is this really how God wants me to live?*

Thankfully, Jesus offers hope and encouragement for those of us who feel overwhelmed and anxious about how we'll get what we think we need. In His famous Sermon on the Mount, Jesus addresses anxiety, worry, and fear about future provision head on:

> "Therefore I tell you, do not be anxious about your life, what you will eat or what you will drink, nor about your body, what you will put on. Is not life more than food, and the body more than clothing? Look at the birds of the air: they neither sow nor reap nor gather into barns, and yet your heavenly Father feeds them. Are you not of more value than they? And which of you by being anxious can add a single hour to his span of life?
>
> And why are you anxious about clothing? Consider the lilies of the field, how they grow: they neither toil nor spin, yet I tell you, even Solomon in all his glory was not arrayed like one of these. But if God so clothes the grass of the field, which today is alive and tomorrow is thrown into the oven, will he not much more clothe you, O you of little faith?

Therefore do not be anxious, saying, 'What shall we eat?' or 'What shall we drink?' or 'What shall we wear?' For the Gentiles seek after all these things, and your heavenly Father knows that you need them all. But seek first the kingdom of God and his righteousness, and all these things will be added to you." (Matthew 6:25-33)

Did you catch that last verse? "Seek first the kingdom of God and his righteousness, and all these things will be added to you."

As Christian writers, speakers, and influencers, we can easily get caught up in the latest digital trends, analytics, online rankings, and other worldly cares. We end up seeking first a coveted endorsement or lofty review. Perhaps we wind up seeking first a keynote speaker slot or a prized position on Amazon.

As we've discussed in earlier chapters, it's important to be strategic and to use our gifts and resources to the best of our ability—but it's also important to measure our motives. As we catch ourselves obsessing over nitty gritty details about how to grow our platform, let's follow those thoughts with a regular heart check—what am I seeking first?

God knows exactly what we need and when we need it. If He thinks we need that review or that speaking engagement, He'll give it to us when He sees fit. If He thinks we need a book with our name on it or a microphone to stand behind, He'll give it to us in His timing. Yes, we must be responsible to actually *use* our gifts, not leave them sitting in the kitchen drawer like my unused flour sifter. But as followers of Christ, our primary job is to focus on Him and His glory, not our own.

RIGHT WHERE YOU ARE

Mr. Wilbur Knight is an elementary school custodian in

Ohio who regularly sings on the job. One day a colleague posted a video to Facebook of Mr. Knight's singing. The video went viral and got picked up by ABC News, who shared the story on December 11, 2017. Mr. Knight then got invited to appear on Good Morning America, where it was shared that he is not on social media, nor does he own any electronic devices. Until his unexpected moment of fame, Mr. Knight didn't even know what it meant for a post to "go viral."

"I just want to touch people's hearts," he said. "I'm going to keep on singing. I'm not going to stop. That's my gift from God."[21]

A week later, pastor and author Alan Cross shared the Good Morning America story on Twitter, along with this comment: "A school custodian sings praise to God where he is, and it is broadcast around the world. Don't try to create a platform for yourself. Just stand where you are and worship Jesus. God will do the rest the way He wants."[22]

That sounds a lot like Jesus' advice in His Sermon on the Mount, doesn't it? Don't worry about the details. Just focus on seeking first His kingdom. God will provide exactly what you need.

THE GRACE TO SAY "NO"

Two weeks before my first traditionally published book released, I got an email from my agent: "Do you have a few minutes to discuss a new publisher's interest in your writing?"

I'll admit that my first thought was, *Wow! My first book hasn't even launched yet, and already someone else is asking about the possibility of a second book?*

It felt good (and a bit strange) to be sought after and pursued as an author—quite different from my first experience knocking on closed doors. There was only one problem: At the time I didn't know if I had a second book in me. The first one—a memoir—had sapped me dry. It had consumed all of my emotional and creative energy. I felt as if I had given it everything I had—what more did I have to offer? Surely any attempts at a second project so soon after the first would be half-baked and end up mediocre. Did I really want to risk letting down my readers, myself, and my God by committing to a project without being fully invested?

But—I did have a publisher reaching out to me, so that was something, right? And I do know *how to* write, so surely I could come up with something passable…right? Even though I didn't have any fully developed book ideas at the time (or partially developed ideas, for that matter), I began to brainstorm options. I was prepared to tell my agent, "Just find out what they're looking for, and I'll see if I can write it."

I went as far as emailing my literary agent with two embryonic ideas—just barely conceived in my mind. He responded by asking if I could develop one of them a bit further, so I took an hour and whipped up a loose outline off the top of my head, then clicked send. I didn't even pray about it first.

Mixed emotions swirled within: excitement over the possibility of another book, but also an obvious check in my spirit that I was rushing headlong into something not meant for me.

Then the Lord brought to mind a blog post I had read a couple of years earlier, written by Christian blogger and artist Aliza Latta. The post was titled, "I Turned Down a Book Deal and This is Why."

On February 9, 2016, Aliza wrote:

"This past October I was offered a book deal. A few days ago, I turned it down. I hadn't sent out a book proposal because I wasn't even considering writing nonfiction. But a publishing house had somehow discovered my blog, liked what they saw, and wanted me to write a book. It's strange to even type that.

When they first emailed me, I think I literally squealed. I was elated, delighted, flattered, exhausted, and shocked. Mostly I couldn't believe it.... Over the next few months the publisher, editor, marketer, and I chatted. They were nothing if not kind. We conceptualized ideas, talked about titles, looked over marketing plans, and did a lot of other book-ish things. I was happily overwhelmed through the whole process, until one week when I started having nightmares.

I am slowly learning that when I have anxiety, she often shows her face through dreams. She sneaks into my head at night, and I wake up feeling sad and confused and lonely. That happened for a week and a half....Since they had offered me the deal, an endless loop had been playing in my mind: *I'm going to be published! I'm going to be published! I'm going to be published!*

I thought being published was the epitome of success. I thought I would have something worthwhile to tell people when they asked me what I did for a living. I thought I would write this book, but I was thinking that for all of the wrong reasons.

I made a promise to myself years and years ago, back when I was seventeen years old, when I began writing a novel. The promise was this:

I will not write a book solely to get published. I will

only write a book if I desperately, relentlessly, urgently need to write the book. I will write because I need to write, not because I hope to be published.

That was a promise I made to my heart, if only to help me come back to the reason why I started writing in the first place. I can't write a book just to write a book. I mean, I could—but I don't want to. It has to be carved so deep within me that I will do literally anything to see its release. I feel this about other projects, other words. I didn't feel that about this one.

I will be 100%, blatantly honest with you: for me, this book wouldn't have been about the words. It would have been about the idea that being published somehow would make me enough.

One day after the anxiety was on full blast in my brain, I woke up and started to fervently pray, using Philippians 4:6 and 7 as my lifeline: "Don't worry about anything, instead pray about everything. Tell God what you need, and thank Him for all He has done. Then you will experience God's peace, which exceeds anything we can understand. His peace will guard your heart and mind as you live in Christ Jesus."

I wanted peace more than anxiety. I wanted my enough-ness to stem from God and not a publishing deal. I wanted Jesus more than anything. So I took my shaky hands and typed an email, clicked send, and didn't have a book deal any longer.

Immediately I wondered if I made a huge mistake.

Would this be my only opportunity to be published? I asked God to confirm that I did the right thing. Not even a half hour later, I felt inexplicable peace.

Everything about this was good. The publishing house was kind, the concept was fantastic, the timeline lovely. It was all good. Which is, I think, why I was feeling so confused. If all of it was lovely, why was I anxious?

When the world offers you something gleaming on a shiny silver platter, it seems foolish to say no. It's so pretty, so tantalizing, so easy to pick up and run with. But in the deep recesses of my heart and soul I knew this shiny morsel wasn't right for me yet. I have to believe that what God has for me—though perhaps not gleaming or shiny or silver—is so much better.

Writing a book to try and prove your worth is not nearly a good enough reason to write a book.

I thought long and prayed hard about this, and the storyteller inside of me wants to write fiction until my fingers bleed. I thought I needed to be a nonfiction writer because that's what was being offered, but I know now that's not true. I thought I needed to accept a publishing deal, because maybe it will be the only one ever offered. But I want to trust God far more than all of this. I need to instead lean into what God has in store for me—and quite honestly, I have no idea what that is.

So there we have it. Maybe foolish. Maybe brave.

You can decide, because the truth is I don't mind which one you choose."[23]

An amazing testimony, isn't it? The Lord used Aliza's example to put my own motives in check. I realized that the excitement I felt over meeting with a new publisher about a future project was not because God had placed a fire in my soul for the work itself—it was actually about the idea of being published again. It was about feeling wanted.

A few days after the email from my agent, our small group at church read from the Gospel of Mark:

> "And rising very early in the morning, while it was still dark, he [Jesus] departed and went out to a desolate place, and there he prayed. And Simon and those who were with him searched for him, and they found him and said to him, 'Everyone is looking for you.' And he said to them, 'Let us go on to the next towns, that I may preach there also, for that is why I came out.'" (Mark 1:35-38, ESV)

Many of us are fighting to get an audience—Jesus had one seeking Him out. He didn't have to post on social media to try to get people to read His message; they lined up, waiting to hear what He had to say. And yet, He chose to walk away from them.

Jesus could have succumbed to the temptation for popularity. He could have let pride inflate His ego: "Everyone is looking for *Me*." Instead, He moved on. Why? To fulfill His purpose: "Let us go on to the next towns, that I may preach there also, for *that is why I came out*" (Mark 1:38, italics mine).

These examples from Aliza and from Scripture helped me to realize that it's okay to say "no." We don't have to take advantage of every single opportunity just because it comes along—in fact, we *shouldn't say* yes to every opportunity if we want to avoid burnout. It's wise to discern what our focus ought to be, and to filter out any activities or engagements that don't align.

FINDING YOUR FOCUS

If you're struggling to determine what your focus should be when it comes to your writing or speaking career, begin with prayer. Seek the Lord's face and His wisdom. Search the Scriptures. Then ask a few trusted friends for their input, and take their advice to heart. Then, as you set out to grow your platform through various means, continue to ask yourself this question before saying yes or no to each opportunity: Am I seeking God's favor, or accolades from the world?

If you could use a "reset" button, perhaps these hymn lyrics will help:

> *Turn your eyes upon Jesus,*
> *Look full in His wonderful face,*
> *And the things of earth will grow strangely dim,*
> *In the light of His glory and grace.*[24]

Once we determine that our focus is to be on Jesus Christ and seeking first His kingdom and righteousness, we can more easily put into practice the topic of the next chapter: trusting Him for the results.

{CHAPTER TWELVE}

TRUST

"Trust in the LORD with all your heart,
and do not lean on your own understanding.
In all your ways acknowledge him,
and he will make straight your paths."
— Proverbs 3:5-6

KATE'S BOOK LAUNCH STORY

Leading up to my first traditionally published book launch, I (Kate) had heard consistent, viable rumors that Amazon pre-orders were a big deal for the success (or lack thereof) of any given product. My understanding at the time was that any orders placed on Amazon prior to the official release date would accumulate, then register as a "sale" on the date that the product switched over from a pre-order to a live listing.

As a result, a large volume of pre-orders, even if they occurred over a span of several days or weeks, could potentially catapult that product into a high sales rank on Amazon—maybe even into the Top Ten of a particular subcategory! Of course I presumed this would do wonders for visibility, credibility, and longevity, all of which translated in my mind to *more sales*.

I had secret visions of people sharing screenshots of my little book as #1 in the memoir category on Amazon, even if that claim to fame only lasted for an hour on my book's release day.

After pouring four years of my life into this project, I wanted to do everything I could to set it up for success. I also didn't want to disappoint my publisher, who had invested countless hours, human resources, and dollars into making this title a reality.

I spent weeks—no, *months*—leading up to release day crafting a strategy that I thought would help the book do well. I created color-coded spreadsheets and enlisted the support of 100 amazing launch team members who committed to reading an early digital copy of the book so they'd be ready to leave an Amazon review on April 2nd, the very first day that the review link was scheduled to go live.

My plan was in place.

Except it didn't exactly happen that way. At all.

What's that verse in Proverbs about how a man plans his course, but the Lord determines his steps? Yeah, that. Apparently the Lord had other plans. Plans that involved my sister texting me at the end of February to tell me that she received an automated email from Amazon stating that her pre-order of my book had shipped! Then the next day, one of my launch team members emailed to say that Amazon had accepted her review already... *What?!* I clicked over to Amazon, and sure enough—my book was no longer listed as available for pre-order. It was just plain *available*. The listing had switched over more than five weeks early without any warning—and without me having time to rally up everyone I knew to pre-order a copy before April 2nd.

My heart sank. I felt as if I had just lost my only window of opportunity to propel my book into the coveted high ranks on Amazon. In my mind at the time, all prospects of my memoir achieving any measure of success had just gone down the drain. I became so flustered and discouraged by the sabotaged plans that I actually cried over it one morning while explaining the situation to my husband. As he so often does when my heart and perspective are in the wrong place, my husband helped me to re-center my focus.

He said, "Kate. This is not a disaster. Your book has been published. It is out there in the world. People are still going to read it. You need to relax."

Though I didn't like hearing it at the time, I knew he was right. I had to trust God to do with it what He pleased, and to get it into the hands of those He had already planned would need it most.

But it's an ongoing fight, this continuous wrestling between pride and humility, action and trust. I'll admit that when I received my first royalty checks after my book's release, I was sorely disappointed by the sales numbers. "I should've done more to promote it!" I lamented. But even this, I later learned, was one more opportunity for me to step back and trust that God knew exactly what He was doing, and that whoever needed the book would read it in His timing.

My friend and fellow author Deidra Riggs shared a helpful perspective with me after her first book released. She said, "I've done my part. I wrote what He told me to write. Now I just sit back and watch my book do its thing. It's like having your kids move out of the house. As a parent you've done what you can to raise them right…now they're on their own. That's how I think about my book. It's out of the house now, and God's gonna do what He wants to do with it."

It's not always a natural or easy perspective to take, but

it's a healthy one—spiritually and emotionally.

SHANNON'S BOOK LAUNCH STORY

I (Shannon) had exactly the opposite experience. I'm not nearly as connected with the writing world as Kate is, and had absolutely no clue about rankings on Amazon, or anywhere else. So unlike Kate, I went into publishing my book with no plan, other than to invite anyone and everyone I knew to come to my launch party, and share news about my book online. How could I go wrong with a plan like this?

To my great surprise, the day before my book was to launch, I started getting notes from friends. "Umm…Amazon is saying that your book is sold out, and it will be two months before they get more…."

"What??!" I replied in horror. When I called my publisher, I learned that it was true. Amazon had pre-sold more books than they had received. I was completely distraught. Here I was, with my megaphone aimed at the World Wide Web, saying, "My book—which I've been telling you about for years—is finally available for purchase!" But when would-be readers went to add my book to their virtual shopping cart, there were no books to be had. Other online stores were out, also. My local bookstore, which hosted my launch party, ran out, too—due to all of the online purchases they received from eager readers.

I was delighted and devastated at the same time. I knew that Bible study groups were planning to use *Control Girl* for their next session, which was starting soon. What if they had no books?

About a week later, I got more bad news. My publisher had received a new order from Amazon, but the order was for more books than had been printed. So they had to *deny Amazon's request*. Please pause and feel the hysterics of my first-time-author heart for a moment. Amazon was requesting more books for would-be readers, and was being told,

"No." I wanted to fling my miniscule-sized self in front of the Amazon giant and wave my hands hysterically, saying, "We'll get you more! I promise!" But of course, there was nothing I could do.

My publisher worked diligently to rectify the problem. A reprint of my book was issued, which delighted me. But then we had to wait for Amazon to reissue their request for more books, which devastated me.

Eventually everyone got their books, but this experience was yet another example of a lesson that God has been teaching me from the first day I set out to write a book on control: He is the One in control; not me. Not you, either. The sooner we get a handle on this lesson, the better.

HOLD AND FOLD

In *Control Girl,* I (Shannon) referenced a parenting book by Tim Sanford called, *Losing Control and Liking It.* Tim shares a principle which is not only helpful for parents and women who want control, but for authors, influencers, and speakers as well.

Tim divides all of life into two categories:

1. What I Can Control
2. What I Can't Control

So what belongs in Category One? What can I ultimately control? Myself. I can control my own efforts, reactions, and attitudes. The rest belongs in the second category.

Certainly, we do have influence over other people—and this book is about how to use that influence in a way that pleases God. But we don't ultimately control whether people buy our books, share our links, listen to our words, or take our messages to heart. However, God does. The reins for every single thing that belongs in Category 2 are tucked safely into God's wise and powerful hands. He truly is in control.

So what should we do with these two categories? Tim Sanford suggests a "Hold and Fold" response. We hold control of the things we can in Category One. This means we write diligently, share our work, and even pay for social media ads to get the word out. But then we fold our hands in surrender to God with all that we can't control in Category Two. We bow before Him, saying, "You take my message, Lord. Use it however You will."

As a self-proclaimed Control Girl, this is really hard for me! I find that I'm constantly trying to grab control of things that belong in Category Two. But this only produces stress, anxiety, frustration, and even anger in me. Would you say that's true of you, too?

Take a moment and list all of the negative emotions that you experience about your influencer ministry. Beside each negative emotion, list the situation(s) prompting these feelings.

Here are some examples to get you thinking:

Emotion	Cause	1 or 2
Jealousy	I don't have nearly as many events scheduled this year as Speaker Y does.	
Anxiety	What if I sell an embarrassingly low number of books, and no one even considers my next book?	
Stress	I'm supposed to get my email subscriber list up to 10,000 but I only have 783.	
Anger	Publisher X didn't accept my manuscript.	
Stress/Anxiety	I keep getting sidetracked with social media. At this rate, I'll never finish preparing my talk on time.	

Now take inventory of your heart and make your own list (or download at www.shannonpopkin.com/influence):

Emotion	Cause	1 or 2

Go back through your list and add which category each one belongs in. Put a "1" beside anything that belongs in the category, "What I Can Control." Put a "2" next to anything that belongs in the category, "What I Can't Control."

In my examples above, the one about being sidetracked with social media deserves a "1." Does your list have any 1's? These are things you *do* have control over. Make a plan to hold yourself accountable. Put your hands to the plow and finish the work God has given you to do.

But I'm guessing your list (like the one I offered) has lots of 2's. These are the outcomes you *don't* have control over. Ask the Lord to help you fold your hands and surrender each of these irritants and frustrations to Him. Pray over each item, and give them to the only One who can do anything about it.

When we heap onto our own shoulders the burden of trying to control Category 1 outcomes, we sag under the pressure. The resulting negative emotions plague our ministries, our personal lives, and our relationship with God.

But when we give God control over the Category 2 things (which only He controls anyway), we find peace, security, joy, and hope. We are able to live freely!

With a spring in our step, we tip our heads back and say, "God, you're in control—which means I don't have to be."

TRUST TESTS

I mentioned back in the chapter on comparison that my first book contract with "Big Christian Publisher" was canceled. The timing for this was uncanny.

Two weeks before my manuscript was due, I called my husband to say, "Honey, I just clicked 'Save'! It's finished! Now I have two weeks to polish!" He suggested we go out for dinner to celebrate. After we made plans, I got off the phone and opened my email. In the time I had been speaking to him, the email arrived, canceling my book.

Immediately I had a sense that this timing was of the Lord. Sure, I cried and felt discouragement, but I couldn't shake the sense that this timing was God-ordained and I could trust Him. In the time that has passed since then, I've only become more convinced that this is true.

God, who knew that this contract was going to be canceled, could have saved me a bunch of work by allowing my contract to be canceled months prior. But He waited for the exact moment that I said, "It's finished!" for the cancellation note to go out. This wasn't just coincidental. I believe that God wanted me to finish that manuscript because He had other plans for it.

And He did! Months later, when I met my knew editor, she casually mentioned that Kregel doesn't usually publish first-time authors who don't have a complete manuscript. I can see why! It's a lot of work to finish a book, and I'm pretty sure I would have never been able to do it without a contract motivating me forward. I believe God gave me the contract with "Big Christian" to get my manuscript ready to send to Kregel. Amazing, right?

There's more. God recently opened my eyes to another part of His plan, which is still unfolding. Kregel's sister organization, Editorial Portavoz, is one of the largest Christian publishers resourcing Latin America. They do an excellent job with translation and creating high quality products. And just this week I learned that they will be translating my book into Spanish! At this point—almost two years after the book has gone into print—Big Christian would have been long finished with the project. But I believe that God also had my future Latina readers in mind, when He placed my book at Kregel.

Isn't He so good?

Oh, how much more peace I have when I trust God to take control, rather than putting the burden of control on my own shoulders. His plans are so much richer and extend so much farther than I can see. Friends, we can trust our God! He is in control. And His plans are so much better than our own.

GOD'S UNLIKELY AUTHOR TEAM

It's so interesting to consider the forty-some authors whom God entrusted with the task of writing the Bible. They didn't *know* they were writing the Bible, of course. But they did know that God was empowering them to do something beyond their own strength.

Compared to the rest of the books in the world, the Bible's influence is like a tsunami next to one gentle, lapping wave. And yet this book, which has been reprinted for centuries and translated countless times, is written by the most unlikely author team.

The first five books of the Bible were written by Moses, a murderer who suffered with a speech impediment (Exodus 2:12, 4:10). Much of the New Testament was written by Paul, another murderer who also suffered from some sort of "thorn in the flesh"—possibly an eye condition (Acts 9:1, 2 Corinthians 12:7). Others who contributed were David, who failed morally (2 Samuel 11:4), and Jeremiah, who was too young (Jeremiah 1:6). The list goes on.

God filled His author team with the most unexpected candidates—and He's still doing so today. God selects those of us who are broken, needy, and weak to do His work. Paul explains why:

> "In order to keep me from becoming conceited, I was given a thorn in my flesh.... Three times I pleaded with the Lord to take it away from me. But he said to me, 'My grace is sufficient for you, for my power is made perfect in weakness.' Therefore, I will boast all the more gladly about my weakness, so that Christ's power may rest on me." (2 Corinthians 12:7-9)

God gave Paul an unremovable thorn for two purposes: 1) It made him humble, which made him useful to God; and 2) It made him weak, which invited God's power.

God's "A-list players" are those who empty themselves of pride of self-sufficiency so they can be filled with His power, not their own. Paul even went so far as to boast about this! He said, "I delight in weaknesses, in insults, in hardships, in persecutions, in difficulties. For when I am weak, then I am strong" (2 Corinthians 12:10).

When you look at the platform beneath your feet, do you feel inadequate and weak? When you look at the neediness of people in the world, do you feel powerless and small? As you face an ocean of need, do you wonder how you could possibly make a difference for God from a platform so small that your toes hang off the edge? If so, welcome to the A-Team. According to Paul, if you feel weak and not up for the task ahead, you should be delighted!

Because you're exactly who God is looking for.

On the other hand, if you feel strong and capable, if your feet are anchored with confidence to a wide, sturdy platform below, you may need to take a step back. You're not quite ready yet. You might be like Peter, who said he would never deny Christ, then did. Or like Samson, who—in his arrogance—didn't realize that God's Spirit had left him. You could need some lifeguard training on how to be weak, not strong. On how to walk by faith, not sight. On how to trust in God, and not yourself.

Don't worry. In His grace and mercy, God will provide every thorn, difficulty, and setback necessary to empty you of yourself, that you might be filled with Him. Like when my contract was canceled. Or like when God allowed Kate's book to be released five weeks early.

God knows exactly how to mold us into the image of His Son—who emptied Himself, wore a crown of thorns, and became the greatest Servant of all. So, how will we respond to our own God-appointed setbacks and thorns? Will we refuse to be humbled? Or will we empty ourselves, invite God's power, and join the A-Team?

IT'S ALL GRACE

As I (Kate) read through Ephesians 2 recently, I almost skimmed over verses 8 and 9 since I already knew them so well: "For by grace you have been saved through faith. And this is not your own doing; it is the gift of God, not a result of works, so that no one may boast." But then the Lord opened my eyes to a surprising revelation—don't these verses apply to my attempts at platform building as well?

Yes, the primary meaning and application of this passage is with regard to the salvation of God's people—we cannot be saved from our sins apart from His amazing grace. No effort or "good" work on our part has anything to do with whether we will be forgiven and welcomed into eternal life with God. Yet how often do I presume that in order to stay in His "good books," I have to perform well? How often—even after being convinced of my sin's pardon on the cross—do I still think I have to be "good enough"? Or maintain a certain standard to retain God's love?

If I take it a step further, I can see that this warped thinking spills into my efforts online. If I'm honest, am I not thinking strategically about how to gain more followers so I can prove myself worthy? Worthy of that book contract, that speaking engagement, that audience? Worthy enough to bring the message God has laid on my heart?

Sometimes I look at my mediocre book sales and scold myself for not *doing more* to promote and market my memoir. But when I sit back and assess the situation, I realize there is absolutely nothing I can do on my own that can win anyone over for any good purpose. Only God can do that. If the Holy Spirit is not working in and through me as well as in the heart of my listener, reader, or follower, nothing of value will happen.

Sure, people and "experts" will try to convince me otherwise. I've fallen for gimmicks and genuine advice alike. I've implemented new social media scheduling techniques, I've paid for more advanced email subscription services, I've updated my website to be more appealing. Shucks, I've even been that person on the other side, advising bloggers and writers about how they can seek to grow their following. I've told them, "When I did this and that, here are the results I saw. It worked for me; you should do it, too." But for what purpose? What is the true motive behind the madness?

I can easily spew forth the "right" answer—I want others to be influenced for Christ. I want the gospel truth to penetrate their hearts and change them. But somewhere along the way the black tar of self has seeped in, covering and darkening my motives.

Instead of focusing solely on Him and His glory, I seek glory for myself. I try to prove myself. I try to *do more*. I want to show others in my sphere of influence that I produce quality work, that I know the steps to success, that I have answers. More than that, I try to make them admire me.

Then, that morning as I read the verses in Ephesians 2, the Word of God put me in my place: It is all grace. It is all the gift of God. Nothing good that has come to me—no good idea, no good opportunity, no good execution, no good result has been a result of my works. Why? So I have no grounds to boast.

If I have any sort of following, if I have sold any books, if my work online or in person has had any influence whatsoever, it is all grace. It is purely His doing, and nothing of my own. I have nothing to boast about or trust in except the grace, goodness, and mercy of my Lord.

TRUST IN THE LORD

As we wrap up our discussion on the topic of using the influence God has given you for His glory, we want to offer Proverbs 3:5-6 as a platform-building blueprint from Scripture:

> "Trust in the Lord with all your heart; lean not on your own understanding; In all your ways, acknowledge Him and He will make your path straight." (NIV, 1984)

I encourage you to commit these verses to memory or display them prominently near your workspace so you'll see them often as you sit down to write, prepare a talk, or post on social media. Yes, we should be strategic. Yes, we should make every effort to distribute as many life jackets as possible with the gifts we've been given. But let's also make every effort to do so while trusting in the Lord for the outcome, not our own ability, eloquence, finesse, or strength.

As you seek to build onto the existing foundation of Christ the Solid Rock, remember: "Unless the Lord builds the house, those who build it labor in vain" (Psalm 127:1). When we labor to build a platform to elevate ourselves, we labor in vain! We've reverted back to life jacket modeling.

Friend, let's not spend our lives laboring in vain. Whatever our confidence level, let's seek to emulate the Apostle Paul, who wrote, "Him we proclaim, warning everyone and teaching everyone with all wisdom, that we may present everyone mature in Christ. For this I toil, struggling with all *His energy* that He powerfully works within me" (Colossians 1:28-29, italics mine).

Your job is not to build your own platform from scratch. It's to build *onto* the foundation that Jesus has already built and extend Christ's reach into the sea of people who need Him. So, remember your focus. Measure your motives. Lean on the One who can make your path straight. Trust Him to use you as a powerful influence for the kingdom as you seek to elevate Jesus, not yourself.

Stand firmly and confidently on the platform God has built for you, and rely on Him to make you the best life jacket distributor you can be, with His help, in His strength, and for His glory.

DISCUSSION GROUP GUIDE

Dear Group Participants,

We're so pleased that you plan to discuss *Influence* with a friend or small group.

We hope this guide will help you to spend your discussion time sharing your own journey, reminding each other of the words of Jesus, and collaboratively refuting the distorted perspective of the world. As those who step onto platforms to shine light and share truth, we mustn't be naïve about the enemy's attacks, which are sure to come. Yet we are far more able to stand firm against temptation and fear when we're standing in a group.

To open the discussion on each chapter, we've provided an "Around-the-Circle Question." These opening questions will evoke answers that are unique to each group member. We encourage you to be supportive, compassionate, and affirming as each person shares their unique experiences.

We've also provided a memory verse from Scripture that corresponds to each chapter. Psalm 119:11 says, "I have stored up your word in my heart, that I might not sin against you." Hiding God's Word in our hearts is a powerful weapon as we fight the sins and temptations that often accompany platform building efforts. We encourage you to make a sincere effort in memorizing these passages. Set realistic goals, and offer to hold one another accountable.

We pray that the Lord would cause your reading of this book, your study of His Word, and your group conversations to bring about much good as you seek to be a light for Him.

CHAPTER 1: TENSION

Memorize: Romans 7:18

1. Around-the-Circle Question: Which do you see yourself as—an underconfident influencer or over-confident influencer? Share a story to support your response.

2. In your own words, describe the tension you feel regarding platform building as a follower of Christ.

3. What lies do you need to stop believing in order to move forward as an influencer for Christ?

4. Depending on your answer to Question #1, share a practical step you can take toward balancing your confidence level (either increasing or decreasing). What changes do you need to make in order to place your confidence where it belongs—in the Lord?

CHAPTER 2: FEAR

Memorize: Psalm 56:3

1. Around-the-Circle Question: Which of these fears do you most identify with? How do these fears keep you from diving head first into the waters of platform building?

   - The fear of being misunderstood

   - The fear of being rejected

   - The fear of being ridiculed

   - The fear of failure

   - The fear of being wrongly perceived

   - The fear of focusing too much on self

- The fear of getting caught up in the numbers

- The fear of not being popular enough

- The fear of not having anything new or interesting or important enough to say

- The fear of silence from the audience

- The fear of seeming self-consumed

- The fear of _____

2. Read 2 Timothy 1:7. What fears do you need to turn over to the Lord?

3. What practical life changes can you make to combat your fears and cling to your God-given identity through Christ?

4. Share about a time when you have experienced "imposter syndrome." What positive strategy can you arm yourself with to prepare for the next time it comes?

CHAPTER 3: CALLING

Memorize: 1 Thessalonians 5:24

1. Around-the-Circle Question: Recall Shannon's story about her dad on the highway. Tell about one of the following:

- A time that you have resembled a "crazy driver, making some noise"

- A time that you have observed another influencer "make some noise" out of selfless concern for others

2. Brainstorm some ways you can actively practice the art of "self-forgetfulness."

3. Read the Parable of the Talents in Matthew 25:14-30. How does this relate to the choices we make regarding gifts we've been given and the calling we've received?

4. Which gifts from God have you been stashing away in your kitchen drawer? What calling from the Lord have you been hiding from? What steps of obedience is He leading you to take in this regard?

CHAPTER 4: FOREWORD

Memorize: Ephesians 2:10

1. Around-the-Circle Question: Share one or more of your responses to the three "foreword" questions about your ministry:

   • What stirred you to share your message?

   • Who affirmed you?

   • What doors did God swing open?

2. What clues has God given you regarding His calling and purpose for your life?

3. Do you most identify with the underconfident or the overconfident influencer described in this chapter? How can identifying your "foreword" help you strengthen any areas of weakness in your ministry?

CHAPTER 5: STRATEGY

Memorize: Matthew 10:16

1. Around-the-Circle Question: What platform-building strategies are you currently conflicted over?

2. Tell about how God used another person to light the lamp of understanding in you. How has God used you to spread light to others?

3. Read Luke 8:4-18. How does it alleviate pressure to note that the emphasis of this parable is not on the sower? In what ways have you been heaping up the burden of control onto your shoulders, trying to manage the outcomes for your ministry? What is one way you can lay this burden down over the coming month?

4. Read Luke 8:18. How do you practice being a good "listener"? How have you seen your ministry either stagnate or flourish, based on how carefully you're receiving God's Word, personally?

5. Read Luke 8:16. What platform has God given you? What unique influence do you have? In what ways have you had disdain for your God-given platform? In what ways have you embraced it?

6. Name at least one way that you can more strategically shine into the darkness.

CHAPTER 6: PRIDE
Memorize: Philippians 2:3

1. Around-the-Circle Question: Which aspects of the writing or speaking life cause you to be most susceptible to pride creeping in? In which specific situations are you most tempted to become a life jacket model instead of a life jacket distributor?

2. What did you find most interesting about the Mystery Sandcastle Masters, who created their art in anonymity and walked away? How would you feel if you did your best work and didn't receive credit for it?

3. Read Genesis 11:1-9. What strikes you most about the builders of the Tower of Babel, who were "trying to make a name for themselves?" In what ways do you see yourself as one of these builders? Is there anything you need to repent of in this regard before the Lord?

4. What changes do you need to make in your life to ensure that you're building God's eternal kingdom on the foundation of the Rock of Jesus Christ, not a temporary sandcastle on the shifting shores of worldly fame?

CHAPTER 7: COMPARE
Memorize: Philippians 4:8

1. Around-the-Circle Question: Tell about a time when you were distracted from the work God has for you because you compared yourself with someone else.

2. In this chapter, Shannon writes about comparison resulting in one of two outcomes: inferiority (leading to shame, jealousy, and insecurity) and superiority (leading to pride, arrogance, and self-exaltation). Share a story about a time when you've experienced one or both of these outcomes.

3. The enemy often uses comparison to lead us into isolation. Have you ever experienced this? The next time you see it happening to you, what can you do to keep yourself from falling into this trap?

4. Read Matthew 20:1-16. How did the first workers hired fall into the comparison trap? What lessons can be learned from this passage?

CHAPTER 8: SIFT

Memorize: Psalm 139:23-24

1. Around-the-Circle Question: What decision or ministry opportunity are you facing that most calls for a "sifting" of your motives?

2. If you used the "Heart Sifter" exercise, share what you discovered.

3. Tell a story about a time when you started something with good intentions, but your motives morphed into selfishness and ungodliness.

4. Take some time to pray Psalm 86:11, either individually or as a group.

CHAPTER 9: SERVE
Memorize: Mark 10:45

1. Around-the-Circle Question: How would you describe your current perspective on platform building? Do you think of it as "gross" and self-serving, or do you view it as an opportunity to serve?

2. How did this chapter challenge your perspective on platform building? Does your position need to be shifted? If so, how?

3. Where or when have you seen someone else using their platform or influence to serve?

4. In what practical ways can you use your platform to elevate others?

5. Read Mark 10:35-45. What stands out to you in this passage? Where do you see yourself in this story?

CHAPTER 10: NETWORK
Memorize: Psalm 27:2

1. Around-the-Circle Question: Tell about a person whom God strategically placed in your life before you even realized you might benefit from knowing them.

2. How do you long for God to use you?

3. In your current setting, how can you make yourself available and open to input?

4. What is one specific way that you can trust God, not yourself, with the strategy of your ministry?

CHAPTER 11: FOCUS

Memorize: Matthew 6:33

1. Around-the-Circle Question: What opportunity or need currently has the most potential of distracting you from the focus God wants you to have?

2. How would you define the primary focus of your current ministry?

3. What "worldly" things are keeping you from the primary ministry focus you identified in Question #2?

4. What did you think about Aliza Latta's story, who chose to turn down a book deal? Is there something in your life that you need the grace to say "no" to?

CHAPTER 12: TRUST

Memorize: Proverbs 3:5-6

1. Around-the-Circle Question: What circumstance or weakness has most forced you to trust in God rather than yourself, as you seek to influence others?

2. If you made a list of What You Can Control and What You Can't Control, share your results.

3. What practical changes do you need to make in your life regarding the items on your list? How can you better make use of the things you can control, and which things do you need to hand over to the Lord?

4. Spend some time praying for the Lord to increase your trust in Him as you seek to elevate His name and influence the world with the truth of the gospel and the love of Christ.

ACKNOWLEDGMENTS

FROM KATE:

I first want to thank the Lord for the opportunity to co-author this book. Thank You for leading and guiding the process and for bringing these efforts to fruition. May it be a fragrant offering to You, and may Your name be elevated above all, now and always.

To Shannon Popkin: It has been an absolute delight to work alongside you on this project. Thank you for your gracious demeanor, enthusiasm, patience, and hard work. This book is what it is because of your gifted contribution. May He use it for His glory!

To my husband, Kagiso: Thank you for encouraging me to keep writing and speaking to the glory of God, and for helping me to discern gifts, goals, and motives along the way. Most of all, thank you for faithfully leading our family by continually pointing us to Christ.

To Kabelo, Dineo, and Caleb: Thank you for your patience and gracious support as I took on yet another project. I love you.

To the Five Minute Friday writing community: Thank you for inspiring me to keep showing up, to keep writing, to keep shining the light of Jesus in a dark world. I am continually in awe of your sincere encouragement. I wrote this book for you.

To Pastor Mark Chanski: Thank you for the sermons and conversations that have helped shape my thinking on this topic, particularly regarding a biblical view of pride, boasting, and humility. You are a blessing.

To the Breathe Christian Writers Conference Committee: Thank you for allowing Ann Kroeker, Shannon, and me to present a breakout session on this topic in 2017.

This book grew out of the conversations leading up to that session, and I'm so grateful it did.

FROM SHANNON:

Thanks to my husband Ken, and our three kids, who are so patient with my "writer's fog" or "speaking hangovers," along with backed up laundry and 9 p.m. dinners. Your sacrifices are not just for me; together we're investing in a Kingdom that has no end.

To the army of Jesus-following speakers, writers, and ministry leaders who have invested in and influenced me, *thank you.*

To my gifted, dedicated, wise ministry leader friends and sisters in the battle, Jackie VanDyke and Rachel Norton: Your passion for God is so contagious! I'm so inspired by the way you serve Him and thankful to be walking beside you. And to Pearl Allard: What a delight to champion and mentor you as you begin this ministry journey. Your humility inspires me.

To my prayer team: I'm so very thankful for the way you faithfully plead my case before the throne. Without His power, my words would be empty.

To Hayley Mullins, Leslie Bennett, Paula Marsteller, Erin Davis, and the rest of the amazing writers and leaders at the Revive Our Hearts blogs: I'm so thankful to be serving beside such humble, dedicated, insightful women of God.

To Cindy Bultema, Robyn Dykstra, and the rest of the Speak Up team: Your coaching and encouragement has equipped me to develop my craft, and emboldened me to speak for Him.

To Janyre Tromp, Kristi Huseby, Laura Dingman, and my other writerly friends: Thanks for being willing to give input and for cheering me on.

To Kate Motaung: I can't imagine a sweeter, more

humble, or more gracious co-author to work with. I admire you even more than when we began.

And most of all, thanks to Jesus, my Savior. Without Your work, there would be nothing to build on. And without Your gifts of the Spirit, there'd be nothing to give. My hope is to follow You closely, and invite others to come along.

ABOUT THE AUTHORS

Kate Motaung is the author of *A Place to Land: A Story of Longing and Belonging, A Start-Up Guide for Online Christian Writers*, and *Letters to Grief.* She is the host of Five Minute Friday, an online community that encourages and equips Christian writers. Connect with Kate at www.katemotaung.com and www.fiveminutefriday.com.

Shannon Popkin loves to blend her gifts for storytelling and humor with her passion for God's Word. Shannon speaks for Christian women's retreats and events, and is a blogging contributor at Revive Our Hearts. Shannon's first book, *Control Girl: Lessons on Surrendering Your Burden of Control from Seven Women in the Bible* released in 2017. Connect with Shannon at www.shannonpopkin.com or by following her on social media.

OTHER BOOKS BY THE AUTHORS

Control Girl: Lessons on Surrendering Your Burden of Control from Seven Women in the Bible

By Shannon Popkin

Join Shannon as she shares what she has discovered about her own control struggles and about God from studying Control Girls in the Bible. Learn how you too can lay down this burden and find rest in surrendering to the One who truly is in control.

A Place to Land: A Story of Longing and Belonging

By Kate Motaung

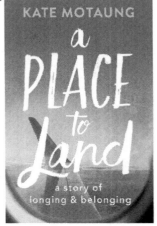

This globe-spanning memoir wrestles with the question, "Where is my home?" Kate watched "home" slip away again and again—through her parents' divorce, two international moves, ten rental homes in ten years, and her mother's terminal battle with cancer. She realizes that no matter where we go or what we do, this world is not our home.

ENDNOTES

1 Kate Motaung, personal tweet, Twitter, April 18, 2018. https://twitter.com/k8motaung/status/987136329866797056 (accessed April 25, 2018).

2 Carl Richards, "Learning to Deal with Imposter Syndrome," *The New York Times*, October 26, 2015. https://www.nytimes.com/2015/10/26/your-money/learning-to-deal-with-the-impostor-syndrome.html (accessed May 29, 2018).

3 "Overcoming Imposter Syndrome," Harvard Business Review, May 7, 2008. https://hbr.org/2008/05/overcoming-imposter-syndrome (accessed May 29, 2018).

4 Kris Camealy, "For Those of Us Wrestling with Imposter Syndrome," KrisCamealy.com, April 2, 2018. http://kriscamealy.com/for-those-of-us-wrestling-with-being-imposter-syndrome/ (accessed May 30, 2018).

5 "Early Training of the Apostle Paul," BibleStudyTools.com. https://www.biblestudytools.com/classics/barnes-scenes-in-life/early-training-of-the-apostle-paul.html (accessed October 17, 2018).

6 John Piper, Sermon: "Take Care How You Listen! Part 1: For Whoever Has, to Him More Shall Be Given," Desiring God, February 15, 1998. https://www.desiringgod.org/messages/take-care-how-you-listen-part-1 (accessed December 12, 2017).

7 John Piper, Podcast: "Incentives to Kill My Love of Human Praise," Desiring God, August 25, 2014. https://www.desiringgod.org/interviews/incentives-to-kill-my-love-of-human-praise (accessed February 22, 2018).

8 Mike Schumann, "Praise Hungry: How to Break the Power of Human Approval," Desiring God, August 31, 2017. https://www.desiringgod.org/articles/praise-hungry (accessed February 22, 2018).

9 "Word of the Year 2013," English Oxford Living Dictionaries. https://en.oxforddictionaries.com/word-of-the-year/word-

of-the-year-2013, accessed February 17, 2018.

10 Stan Schroeder, "And the Oxford Dictionaries Word of the Year Is…'Selfie,'" Mashable, November 19, 2013. https://mashable.com/2013/11/19/oxford-dictionaries-word-of-the-year-is-selfie/#wtipWLyWBaqh (accessed February 17, 2018).

11 Kyle Idleman. *The End of Me.* (Colorado Springs: David C. Cook, 2015). p. 75.

12 https://twitter.com/lorewilbert (accessed December 19, 2017).

13 Isaac Watts, "When I Survey the Wondrous Cross," 1707. Lyrics accessed from Timeless Truths: Free Online Library, https://library.timelesstruths.org/music/When_I_Survey_the_Wondrous_Cross/ (accessed December 19, 2017).

14 Kevin DeYoung, "The Fetid Pool," The Gospel Coalition, January 27, 2010. https://www.thegospelcoalition.org/blogs/kevin-deyoung/the-fetid-pool (accessed September 3, 2018).

15 Trevin Wax, "Blogging about My Book: Self-Promotion, Stewardship, and More . . .", The Gospel Coalition, February 7, 2011. https://www.thegospelcoalition.org/blogs/trevin-wax/blogging-about-my-book-self-promotion-stewardship-and-more/ (accessed July 12, 2018).

16 Tony Reinke. *12 Ways Your Phone is Changing You.* (Wheaton: Crossway, 2017).

17 ibid.

18 ibid.

19 From two separate Facebook graphics on Ann Voskamp's public Facebook page: https://www.facebook.com/AnnVoskamp/photos/a.369461463066034/2092273360784827/, July 19, 2018 (accessed September 3, 2018); https://www.facebook.com/AnnVoskamp/photos/a.369461463066034/1881806301831535, February 6, 2018 (accessed September 3, 2018).

20 Dan Darling, "Some Thoughts on Writers and Platform," Daniel Darling, April 19, 2017. http://ht.ly/EGo650aXsRs (accessed August 23, 2018).

21 Eliza Murphy, "Singing elementary school custodian spreads cheer in the hallways with voice," ABC News http://abcnews.go.com/Lifestyle/singing-elementary-school-custodian-spreads-cheer-hallways-voice/story?id=51717774, (accessed December 19, 2017).

22 Alan Cross, personal tweet, Twitter, December 18, 2017. https://twitter.com/AlanLCross/status/942754246344298496, (accessed December 18, 2017).

23 Aliza Latta, "I turned down a book deal and this is why," Aliza Latta, February 9, 2016. https://alizalatta.com/aliza-latta/i-turned-down-a-book-deal-and-this-is-why (accessed April 27, 2018). Quoted with permission.

24 Helen H. Hemmel, "Turn Your Eyes Upon Jesus," 1922. Public Domain.

18269782R00093

Made in the USA
Middletown, DE
06 December 2018